CONTENTS

LIST OF FIGURES

LIST OF TABLES

FOREWARD TO THE THIRD EDITION

It has been a privilege and an honour to write this book. Linguistics is not just work but also a hobby and being able to write the kind of book that someone may randomly stumble upon and leaf through to discover a whole new hobby of their own is indeed a privilege. It's also an honour because I walk in heavy shoes. Robert Trask wrote the first two editions of this book, and his expertise and knowledge led him to produce a popular and informative read. My hope for this third edition is that it will uphold his legacy of enticing new generations of budding language scholars to the field, stir up interesting dinner conversations and inform as well as entertain. I have chosen to rewrite this book entirely because the field has changed so much over the past 20 years, since the second edition saw the light of print.

One important caveat is that by its very nature, this book does not provide an exhaustive or even a comprehensive view of linguistics as a research field. There are many interesting areas, questions and insights that have been left out to accommodate the "basic" nature of the text. There are probably also biases in my own leanings and interests that will have inevitably steered the contents away from some areas and more heavily towards others.

I followed Trask's original structure of having nine chapters, starting and ending on similar chapters but changing a few chapters in between. Similarly to Trask, I also bold key jargon linguistics terms and explain them within the text. New areas added in this book cover the relationship between language and computers (which has a chapter of its own) and making up words (which receives more attention than in Trask's versions). The chapters on grammar and on how language varies have seen major revisions, largely because of changes in how we approach those fields today. I also follow Trask in adding a section at the end of each chapter with additional suggested resources for those left wanting more, and these resources have been chosen to include podcasts and videos, in keeping with our modern tendency to consume information through different mediums. I have attempted to write this book in an informal, conversational and approachable style. There are two exceptions to this. First, the layout of language examples is given in a conventional way akin to how they might be given in academic texts, numbered and indented from the main text. A second exception is the addition of references and sources throughout the text, giving credit to those whose work I draw on.

By the time you finish reading this book, you will similarly discover (or rediscover, if you are familiar with Trask's book) that you knew much more about grammar than you realised and you will know the truth about Eskimo words for snow, and hopefully agree that just about any aspect of our identity can be performed, from gender to sexuality and race. In writing this book, I have tried to stay close to (real) language examples and away from any specific theories. The content included draws on as much recent research as possible in a bid to present the field of language study from a modern and fresh perspective, showing not just the insights that we are uncovering today but also peering at the questions left to answer in the future.

ACKNOWLEDGEMENTS

I am grateful to Louisa Semlyen for entrusting me with this third edition, for her advice and her generous lunches and for her faith in my ability. I also thank Heather Doquiatan for leading the editorial process so smoothly and efficiently and for guiding me towards completion.

My sincere appreciation to Miriam Meyerhoff for fruitful discussions and for sharing her research with me, and to Jessie Burnette and Joe Ulatowski, who read parts of this book. Some of the most helpful assistance can come from people we never meet face to face, and I want to acknowledge my many colleagues who shared their work and insights with me, including our wonderful librarian Maria McGuire, who tirelessly chased every article or book I sought, always with cheerful enthusiasm and astounding efficiency.

I am also grateful to my research assistant, Serrano Lorenzo, who read the whole book. My dear friend and mentor Laurie Bauer also read it in its entirety, offering many helpful suggestions. This book also benefitted from advice and feedback provided by several anonymous referees.

The New Zealand Royal Society Marsden Fund facilitated (in part) this opportunity and provided financial support.

Writing a book of this type constitutes a selfish act, fuelled by the arrogance that your view of (in this case) language is sufficiently inspired and exciting to draw in those who perhaps don't realise the field exists in the first place. Looking back to how my own curiosity was first sparked and maintained over the years, I am grateful to my professors and supervisors, Allan Scott, Donna Starks, Frantisek

Lichtenberk and Jim Miller for enticing me into the world of linguistics.

As always, my husband Paul James graciously and ever-so-enthusiastically cheered me on, reading this book cover to cover and allowing himself to be drawn in endless conversations about its contents. I am equally indebted to him for providing several illustrations (Figures 1.1, 2.2, 7.1, 7.2).

1

LANGUAGE … LANGUAGE EVERYWHERE

Language is one of humankind's most remarkable achievements. It is an achievement because it's vital in allowing us to connect with one another and to transmit our knowledge and culture from one generation to the next. It's remarkable because we think no other species on earth has anything quite like it, and we cannot imagine a modern world like we have today without it. It's also remarkable in the sheer diversity of features we find across the roughly 7,000 languages spoken across the globe today.

In this book, I am going to try and convince you of these things and of a few more. Some of us are very attached to our languages and have strong opinions about how they should be spoken or written. We view the very idea that language matters as a huge understatement. Others never think much about language at all. It's just there. Some readers will be multilingual, juggling a few languages, others monolingual, having just one. For some, the notion that language will inevitably change and flex seems preposterous and disappointing, while for others, flouting old rules is exciting and invigorating.

Despite these differences, there is one thing we all share, which is that every single one of us uses language. Moreover, we do so every day. Whether through a screen, a website, a billboard, a podcast, a menu, a TV show, a book or a newspaper, we still consume a lot of language because language is … well, everywhere. If you think about it, it is impossible to go through your day without bumping into some form of language, be it text language, spoken language, signed language or written language. Language is used to get things done, order our morning coffee, yell at the ever-increasing traffic while humming to our favourite tunes, greet friends, do work, joke

DOI: 10.4324/9781003621485-1

around, spill gossip, make appointments, break promises, sign contracts, apologise, flirt, vent, complain and relax, and some of us even talk in our sleep.

This book attempts to unpack a whole host of features and characteristics observed in different types of languages, showing that the field whose business is to document and investigate language – **linguistics** – is a thriving area of research, full of excitement and fascinating discoveries. Because we are all language users, it is tempting to think everyone is an expert too, which sometimes gives rise to myths, some of which I hope to dispel here.

The very label of the field itself is commonly misunderstood. You will meet many a linguist who is fed up with being asked how many languages they speak or which language they teach. But asking a linguist how many languages they speak is as absurd as asking a vet how many pets they have (Figure 1.1). At the same time, language is so vast and ubiquitous that it might seem difficult to know where to begin.

Figure 1.1 Asking a linguist how many languages they speak is as absurd as asking a vet how many pets they own

Illustration credit: Paul D. James

This book covers more technical, inward-looking areas of language, like how we get new words, how we string words together and how we begin to analyse meaning. It also covers places where language interacts with other fields of inquiry. These outward-looking topics consider how language varies across people and social groups (sociolinguistics) and time (historical linguistics), connections between language and the brain (language acquisition, psycholinguistics) and interactions between language and computers (computational linguistics). These are not the only connections which language makes with other fields, but in the interest of space and the desire to limit this book to 'the basics', decisions had to be made about what to include and what to leave out.

WHAT IS HUMAN LANGUAGE REALLY LIKE?

Before we can even begin with studying language, we ought to ask. Is human language really unique to us, or do other species have language too? After all, other living organisms have been shown to possess systems of communication. Take, for example, the humble bacteria that live in our gut. It turns out that these bacteria can transmit messages to our brains through a series of chemical reactions and thereby affect the development of certain nervous system processes, including certain diseases (Lu et al., 2024). Sure, this is a kind of communication, but is it language?

It's not trivial to ask whether language is uniquely ours. The value of asking this question lies in growing our own understanding of what we mean when we think of language as we know it. In the 1960s, pondering this very question led Charles Hockett to devise an extensive list of **features** designed to unpack and capture the inner characteristics of human language (Hockett, 1960).

One of these relates to **cultural transmission**, which is the property that stipulates language to be a culturally transmitted tool. We learn language initially from our parents or guardians, and later from peers, but in general, from other humans in our midst. It is true that other species transmit their communication systems to one another in a similar way, for instance, birds learn to imitate the types of songs which other birds of the same species make. However, this influence is not crucial in the same way for other species as it is for us humans. It's been found that birds raised in isolation will also exhibit songs, albeit odd-sounding ones. In contrast, children raised in the wild do not develop proficiency in human language if left on their own. And if discovered much later in their lives, typically beyond puberty, they never achieve it even with instruction and guidance once assimilated within a particular community.

While human languages share many of Hockett's features with communication systems of other animals, especially primates, no other species seems to have all of them together. This makes human language unique. Over the years, Hockett came up with different lists of features, one had 13, another 16, the number is not significant, what is important is that these features have become a central lens for understanding the fabric of human language, as well as a point of comparison with communications systems of other species. Let's consider a few other features and look at comparisons with other communication systems.

DISPLACEMENT

Moving to more exciting species than bacteria, take, for instance, the honeybee. Honeybees employ a tail-wagging dance consisting of distinct unit moves, which map out a path towards the source of nectar. Moreover, their dance can vary depending on the species, which is akin to **dialect** variation in human language, think Austrian German and Swiss German (both are German, yet German with differences). Honeybees use various features in their dance to signal different aspects of the nectar. The time it takes to complete certain segments indicates the distance to the nectar, the level of enthusiasm corresponds to the quality of the nectar, and the orientation of the dance indicates the direction of the nectar with respect to the position of the sun.

It seems astounding that such a small organism can communicate so accurately about things that are not present right there at the time of the interaction, a property that Hockett termed **displacement**. While honeybees share displacement with us, they cannot communicate about any old thing that is not present at the time of interaction; they can't tell us if it's going to rain or not, nor can they make up stories about unicorns, dinosaurs or Santa Claus. The extent to which honeybees have displacement is limited specifically and exclusively to the location of nectar. Human language has displacement on a much larger scale.

DUALITY AND PRODUCTIVITY

But how does communication happen in the first place? Doing a dance is something that is registered visually, you have to see it. The visual channel is just one way in which other species 'talk' to each other. According to Stephen Anderson's (2020) meticulous documentation of animal communication systems, species can communicate through many different channels. Some species communicate through olfactory signals or smell, as observed in ants, moths, mice and lemurs. Others use ultrasound, such as bats and dolphins. Elephants use infrasound ranging between 1 and 20 Hz, which is below human hearing abilities but which can travel more than 10 km. Some species of fish use electric fields. Many species leverage multiple channels at the same time, not just one.

Another common form of communication is the use of sound, employed by birds of various kinds, prairie dogs, domesticated cats, Arctic foxes, chimps and so on. Sound is also a primary means of communication for human languages. In human languages, the majority of sounds are produced by ejecting air from our lungs to articulate **phones** like the first sound in *to* (let's write this as T), the first sound in *moo* (M) and the first sound in *see* (S).

Some languages also produce sounds by sucking air inwards to make click sounds, as heard in the language name of *Xhosa* or the tutting sequence *tsk!tsk!*. There are also human languages that use whistling sounds, like the language spoken by the Hmong people at the base of the Himalayas or Silbo Gomero, a whistled version of Spanish spoken in the Canary Islands. These sounds allow speakers to transmit messages as far as 8 km away.

Sounds can be combined in sequences that become associated with meanings. In English, we can distinguish many different words which only differ through one single sound, such as *lap*, *tap*, *nap*, *map* and *rap*. By changing the sound that the letter L represents to the sound of a T, N, M or R, we get new words. Notice that spelling happens to match the sounds in these examples, but that is not always the case; more on that soon. These sounds do not have any meaning of their own, but once combined with other sounds, they suddenly do. This property was termed by Hockett **duality of patterning**, or duality for short.

Unfortunately, English spelling is not helpful in illuminating what a word sounds like, as famously captured by the made-up example *ghoti,* which is said to be pronounced as *fish*: *gh* is pronounced as F following words like *tough* and *rough*, *o* is uttered like it is in *women*, and *ti* is said as it is in words like *lotion* and *nation*. (Incidentally, the attribution of this example to the language commentator and playwright George Bernard Shaw is a myth; its origin comes from the publisher Charles Ollier.)

Such inconsistencies between spelling and pronunciation have given rise to the **International Phonetic Alphabet** (IPA), a special writing system devised specifically to write down speech. The IPA, as it is known in short, is extremely handy for many people, from language learners – that is what you sometimes see in square brackets in learner dictionaries – to speech language therapists.

Nevertheless, the words above demonstrate that by changing one single sound, we are able to derive whole new forms and meanings, and this kind of **productivity** allows human languages to devise large vocabularies.

It is important to note here that sound is not the only means employed by human languages. There is also gesture, which is found in all languages to a greater or lesser degree, and hand signing, used as the primary channel of communication by Sign Languages (more on Sign Languages later).

ARBITRARINESS

It is fun to turn these ideas around and consider the way in which us humans imitate the sounds that animals make. In essence, we simply vocalise what we hear, the fancy term for this being **onomatopoeia**. But here's the rub. In English, mice say *squeak-squeak*, dogs bark *woof-woof*, roosters go *cock-a-doodle-doo* and ducks *quack-quack*. In Romanian, mice go *chiţ-chiţ*, dogs say *ham-ham*, roosters go *cucuriguuu* and ducks *mac-mac*. In French, it's different again: *cui-cui, ouf-ouf, cocorico-cocorico, coin-coin*.

These observations nicely illustrate that just like what we say (**production**) differs wildly across languages, what we hear (**perception**) does too. Unless of course, mice, dogs, chickens and ducks are highly talented in varying their sounds and messing with our brains.

In general, most words have no direct link between their form and meaning. The word we use for the four-legged animal that barks and many humans like to keep as a pet happens to be *dog* in English, *kurī* in Māori, *câine* in Romanian and *inu* in Japanese. The phrase 'happens to be' is deliberate here because there is no connection between forms and their meanings; the link is **arbitrary**. It is not that cases of **iconicity** (pairings between forms and meanings) do not exist, because they certainly do (Winter et al., 2017). Examples include the onomatopoeia examples above and associations between forms like *bouba* and round objects, *kiki* and sharp shapes and *teeny* and small items. But the point is that Hockett dismissed these as trivial and insignificant, emphasising the arbitrary nature of the lexicon. However, this is currently an area of intense scrutiny with new experiments involving speakers of completely unrelated languages exhibiting some strikingly similar associations. Many questions remain about the importance of iconicity, and we are still trying to understand just how much arbitrariness is found in human language.

There are several key differences between the range of sounds that other species utilise and the arrangement of sounds found in human language. One is the sheer number of **words** (Chapter 2) found in the repertoire of each species. According to Anderson, the highest number of distinct vocalisations found in any other species studied is 40. Compare that with more than 500,000 listings for English in the *Oxford English Dictionary* or with the astounding 21-volume *Historical Dictionary of the Arabic Language*. Incidentally, this Arabic dictionary entered the *Guinness Book of World Records* in December 2024 for being the largest linguistic project globally, involving more than 500 researchers and nearly 200 proofreaders and reviewers.

Secondly, the vocalisations encountered in say bird song or other forms of communication have fixed meanings, leaving little room for interpretation. For example, bird species can sing many different songs, combining the same basic elements in slightly different ways, and some have a whopping repertoire of hundreds of song patterns. However, the interpretation of such songs is roughly the same, either denoting territorial dominance or advertising mating opportunities. Similarly, the vervet monkeys exhibit a finite set of vocalisations used to warn against potential threats, such as the sighting of an eagle, leopard or snake. But here also, the interpretation of sounds is contextually fixed.

In English (and English is not unique in this sense, it is just convenient for illustrative purposes), a single word can have a vast array of interpretations depending on the context. *Coffee* can refer to a particular jar in my kitchen, it can denote a type of drink, it can express an activity like 'going for coffee', it can be an invitation or question 'do you want a coffee?' or even reference a type of meeting which, weirdly, may not involve coffee at all.

OPEN-ENDEDNESS

There is also our impressive ability to both combine words in new sequences never heard before and decode novel combinations never encountered before. This **open-endedness**, another feature of human language, can be both frustrating and entertaining, again, depending on context. The chimpanzee Nim Chimpsky (yes, a parody of the well-known linguist Noam Chomsky, a staunch critic of ape studies) and the bonobo Kanzi rose to great public fame by purportedly being able to produce novel sentences. But alas, the initial excitement was short-lived as the data they produced did not stand up to scrutiny.

All this is not to say that other species cannot successfully manipulate the context of communication. For example, it has been observed that in some species of primates, a female engaged in copulation with a non-dominant male in the group can control the loudness of her vocalisations when in the earshot of a dominant male. However, the nature and extent of such manipulation are isolated in other species, while in human languages, they constitute the backbone of everyday conversation. Consider the following examples:

(1) *Him: You look nice tonight.*
Her: I have a headache.

(2) *Mother: You look nice tonight.*
Daughter: I am just going to Eva's. God. [rolls eyes]

It takes a very good grasp of the situation and considerable inference to accurately interpret the different pairs involving a sentence like *You look nice tonight*, because the range of possibilities varies from context to context.

The unpredictability and creativity of human language, the vast array of possibilities of interpretation and our inclination to use language in dynamic, innovative ways, forever adding words and tinkering with their meanings constitute powerful reasons why we believe that language 'as we know it' is ours and ours alone.

SIGNED LANGUAGE

Learning to speak your first language is something that only parents remember. Well, unless your parents happen to be **language acquisition** researchers trying to understand this process, and they have fastidiously recorded everything you have ever said, analysed it and written it in academic articles for posterity to see. For most of us, parents will only have patchy memories, maybe a first word, a funny way of pronouncing the word *shoe* (one of my children used to say *ush*), and the odd anecdote of an endearing misunderstanding. It takes roughly four to six years to get there (Chapter 7), which is – depending on who you ask – both remarkably quick (scholars) and painfully slow (parents).

But imagine that your child is Deaf and cannot speak at all. Unless you are also Deaf yourself, they are going to be learning a Sign Language completely different from your language and one you will also be learning alongside them so that you can communicate with each other. Now consider Nicaragua in the 1970s. It's 1977, and a school opens in Managua that caters to a group of 25 children who are all Deaf but born to hearing (and speaking) parents. The country has no Deaf community to speak of, let alone any awareness of how to best serve its needs. Deaf children are taught to lip-read Spanish, with little success. However, they are allowed to communicate using their made-up gestures on the school bus and on the playground. Fast forward to 1979 and 25 becomes 100. A year later, a vocational school opens close by, where many of the children follow on within their cohorts. By 1983, these schools are serving the needs of over 400 Deaf students and so, a community is born.

This community of children would go on to rapidly develop a fully-fledged language, with no starting point and entirely ad hoc, a language we now call Nicaraguan Sign Language. Nicaraguan Sign Language constitutes one of the most impressive feats in language creation throughout human history, created from need, creativity and a deep desire for social connection. Step aside Esperanto and take note. Apparently, making up a language is child's play.

You may have heard of Baby Sign, a collection of gestures taught to young infants and their carers to alleviate the frustrating pace of learning a first language. But don't be fooled: while there might be some similarities between Baby Sign and Sign Languages, there is a world of difference between them too. Sign Languages are much more than iconic gestures; they are fully fledged languages, with unique lexicons, word formation processes and grammar, just like any other language (Alexander & Major, 2020).

Another interesting observation about Sign Languages is that they are typically not written down. There are some symbols and conventions for writing Sign Language, but the most common way to represent this kind of language on a page, say in a dictionary, is by pictures or videos. In practical terms, what that means for Sign Language speakers is that when they are required to learn to write, they must do so in a foreign language. Unsurprisingly, this is neither easy nor quick to learn, which leads to stigma and marginalisation of Deaf speakers in mainstream culture, where their multilingualism is misunderstood.

Moreover, like other languages, Sign Languages have their own history and genetic relationships. And these may surprise you. For example, being able to speak Australian English does not mean you can understand or use Australian Sign Language (Auslan). Although Auslan, New Zealand Sign Language (NZSL) and British Sign Language (BSL) are genetically related and share a common ancestor, namely Old British Sign Language, American Sign Language has a distinct origin (McKee & Kennedy, 2000).

The origin of American Sign Language lies with Indigenous Signing practices, which kicked off in (what we now call) America before Laurent Clerc, a Deaf French schoolteacher, opened the first public school for Deaf children. Eventually, BSL also arrived on American shores during colonisation. Today, American Sign Language is thought to have combined elements from Indigenous Signs and French Sign Language with some influence from British Sign Language.

In contrast, NZSL and Auslan both took off only following colonisation, once an older version of BSL was already transported to Aotearoa New Zealand and Australia, respectively. Contact between speakers of the varieties also remained high. This is how NZSL and BSL ended up being mutually intelligible languages, in the same way that New Zealand English and British English are. However, they remain separate **dialects** (or varieties); for example, NZSL uses many signs for concepts borrowed from Māori (the Indigenous language of the country), which are completely absent from BSL.

As there are Deaf people all over the world, so too we find Sign Languages in all corners of the globe, each with its own history, each serving the needs of its respective community.

SPOKEN LANGUAGE

If you grew up learning a language other than Sign Language, you probably did so by speaking it. It sounds absurd to even state this, but it is true. Maybe it is because we speak with such ease and so frequently that we rarely notice it. Or maybe because we remember our struggle in learning how to write, a skill many of us seem to keep developing throughout our lives, starting with formal schooling and beyond, if we are lucky enough to attend higher education. Comparatively, we do not recall learning how to speak (our first language). Whatever the reason, speech seems to be less valued than writing, and until recently, it was also not thoroughly studied.

It is sobering to write down a conversation and take stock of how it looks on the page. Here is an exchange recorded and transcribed in Wellington, Aotearoa New Zealand, in the late 1990s. This excerpt is part of a language collection (a **corpus**), gathered systematically and specifically by a team of linguists for the purpose of analysing New Zealand English (Holmes et al., 1998). I will refer to the speakers as A and B rather than using their real names, in order to protect their privacy.

(3) A: what sort of law is she gonna do
B: she wants to be a family court judge
A: yeah? get involved in all the family disputes that'd be quite hard

B: it's well yeah I think so too it's not in the area that I'd like to get involved in I sort of think that my oh just the way I've been brought up you sort of think people's private affairs are private

A: be quite yeah

B: you shouldn't get involved but in HER mind there's always gonna be a family court judge deciding disputes custody and stuff and she said that in the c in the course of doing her degree she's read some really crappy decisions

How strange it is to read speech! In this example, the transcriber deliberately refrains from including punctuation, except for the question mark denoting upward intonation. This is done to avoid imposing a grammatical breakdown into phrases and sentences before any linguistic analysis had taken place. In fact, splitting running speech into sentences has proven impossible because even linguists cannot agree where to draw sentential boundaries. Instead, grammarians agree to use the concepts of a **clause** (more on this in Chapter 3) and of combinations of clauses, rather awkwardly called a **clause complex** (Miller & Calude, 2020).

As the excerpt above illustrates, spontaneous, unplanned conversation is not structured around full stops and commas. It flows liberally and incrementally like beads on a string, across speaker turns, which sometimes overlap.

The information chunks are typically short: *get involved in all the family disputes* is one chunk, *that'd be quite hard* is another. There is not much explicit grammatical connection between them, beyond words like *it* or *that/this* pointing back to previous mentions. In writing, this might be rephrased as *Getting involved in all the family disputes would be quite hard* or *It would be quite hard to get involved in all the family disputes*. But that requires planning and editing, neither of which is available in conversation, unless it has been previously rehearsed.

Chunks are interrupted by false starts and restarts, *in the c in the course* and *my oh*, hedges and time-buying elements (**discourse markers**) like *sort of, and stuff* and *I mean, well yeah*. Addressees signal that they are still listening by small linguistic encouragements like *mm, yeah and quite*.

The narrative is jointly constructed, and speakers must simultaneously decode what they are being told, think of a response, formulate it and then deliver it in a reasonable time. There is so much to think about and pay attention to.

In their book, *The Language Game*, Morten Christiansen and Nick Chater describe language as a 'game of charades' in which speakers and listeners are playing together, coding and decoding each other's messages. As soon as one of the 'players' is not paying attention or trying anymore, everyone loses, game over.

This constant process creates a 'bottleneck of attention', which leads to 'just-in-time language production'. According to them, we produce (on average) about 150 words a minute or 300–350 syllables a minute. It seems nigh impossible that the current record holder for English can roll out a whopping 667 words per minute. But even for us regular speakers, spontaneous conversation requires an astounding amount of anticipation because just-in-time speaking pushes us to get ready for our turn before the current speaker has actually finished theirs.

No scenario highlights this anticipation better than a heated argument with a close family member or partner. Oh yes, you know you are no longer listening to your interlocutor's contributions, you are much too busy preparing your next rebuttal to be paying attention or take in their points. Arguments are more like barely-if-at-all-in-time production. Either way, emotional conversations aptly illustrate the cognitive burden that the constant back-and-forth exchange takes on the human brain. Luckily, not all conversations and certainly not all language exchanges involve a hot-blooded emotional duel.

Some speech is less emotive, for example, a university lecture or work presentation. Other speech may not elicit a direct response at all; it's more like a one-way channel. Think TV or radio news broadcasts. Yes, there are listeners, millions of them perhaps, but no one is responding to the speech they just heard. Yelling back to your TV or radio does not count because the speaker cannot hear you, and there are no conversational turns or jointly constructed discourse. Depending on the program, the speech can be highly scripted, probably not produced by the reader of the broadcast but by a news-writer, and it is likely read from a prompt. Other forms of scripted speech include dialogues in movies and presidential speeches. These forms of communication still count as speech, but their language is very different from that observed in casual conversation. In some cases, they might as well be writing.

WRITTEN LANGUAGE

In complete contrast to conversation, we have carefully planned and heavily edited writing. Academic books, legal contracts and highbrow newspaper articles are all examples of turn-free, poured-over, revised and reworked, manicured language.

This language is often complex, informational and precise. Here is an excerpt from the book contract I signed together with my publisher, as our joint agreement to produce this book.

(4) You agree to write, compile or edit the Work (including, for the avoidance of doubt, all of the constituent parts listed in the Core Terms) and deliver it to the Publisher by the Due Date in a suitable electronic format specified by the Publisher.

Can you imagine anyone speaking like this? Hopefully not. The purpose of such agreements is to set out clear guidelines for everyone's responsibilities. Contracts are essentially formal promises whose function is to spell out the promise as concisely as possible, while avoiding ambiguities to eliminate potential future disagreements. This function drives the language towards clarity and specificity, while also trying to minimise wordiness. In practice, this leads to **jargon** (specialised and technical language) like *the Work* and *Core Terms*, and complex grammar with nested phrases, for example, *a suitable electronic format specified by the Publisher.*

Nevertheless, not all written language is quite like this. Diary entries are traditionally written down, though they could also be sound recorded. But they contain unplanned, unedited language which is more similar to spontaneous conversation than to academic writing or legal language. Scribbled notes left on your desk to remind you to do a certain task are also different from these. There is a continuum from speech to writing, on which spontaneous, unplanned speech gradually morphs and changes, depending on function, content and audience to something that looks very formal, complex and highly edited.

For decades, written language enjoyed special status in at least two ways. First, people who could read and write were associated with higher social standing. Second, written language itself was seen as more eloquent, well-formed and 'proper' or 'correct' when compared to speech. Written language was the yardstick by which spoken language often fell short. Some linguists (Noam Chomsky was one) also saw it as capturing the (idealised) Universal Grammars that (idealised) speakers had inside their heads and thus contained the key to language itself.

However, the written language bias began to turn with the advent of a paradigm shift in the field of linguistics, a shift towards authentic language data as a source of study, a method which came to be known as **corpus linguistics**. Accessing actual speech by leveraging technology, increased computational power and storage capability only accelerated the interest in spoken language. These advances allowed such studies to flourish as researchers began to access what-was-actually said rather than what-we-remember-as-having-been-said. This is a particularly positive development because spoken language can provide a more accurate window into language in-the-wild (unedited, raw and off the cuff).

Humans are notoriously bad at remembering word-for-word accounts or remembering much at all sometimes. It has been noted that otherwise perfectly capable speakers may not even remember the language in which a given interaction took place. But reliable and cheap recording technology changed all that. Because unplanned speech provides direct clues to the nature of language in action, it is also where **language change** comes in more readily and often, where it comes in first (Chapter 6). In modern society, nowhere is language change more consciously called out than on social media platforms.

VIRTUAL LANGUAGE

Here is an old question with a new twist. Do we spend more time speaking and listening or writing and reading? The story used to be that we speak and listen far more than we read and write, even for those of us who write for a living. Until social media came in that is. Now we just don't know. According to Naomi Baron's book *Always On: Language in an Online and Mobile World*, we are 'always on' our devices, fuelled by fear-of-missing-out (FOMO), we constantly check messages on WhatsApp, Signal and Messenger and scroll through Instagram, BlueSky or Facebook.

Media fuels the view that exposure to social media language makes everyone less literate, ironically missing the fact that such language is typically *read* from a screen (Calude, 2023). It is true that there is also plenty of content in video format, but writing often dominates (at least for now). One main concern regarding social media language is that virtual language is grammarless, comma-less, ridden with misspellings and decidedly *less*. New words are coming in unconstrained (Chapter 2), and there are concerns that, especially young people can no longer write 'proper L-ish [insert your favourite language here]' anymore or be understood by older generations. (Were they ever understood?) Adding insult to injury, this ill-fated newspeak appears to be spreading outside the online world into regular conversations and, worse still, into 'proper' writing. Some people revel in using **hashtags** in speech, along with meme references, abbreviations and leaving sentences unfinished. Because internet. Good thing we all agree on everything. No wonder we are no longer speaking to each other and prefer interacting with ChatGPT and other AI assistants instead (Chapter 8).

Yet, compare the excerpts of speech and writing we saw earlier with the following LinkedIn post produced by *The Guardian* on 14 January 2025, discussing Meta's decision to eliminate fact-checkers on its platforms. The formatting is exactly as in the original post on LinkedIn. Which type of language does it resemble best, speech or writing?

(5) When Mark Zuckerberg announced dramatic changes to Meta's social platforms last week – including Facebook, Instagram and Threads – he admitted: "We're going to catch less bad stuff."

But what will be the real-world consequences of these changes?

For Today in Focus, Jesse Stiller, a factchecker, tells Michael Safi about the impact on his work with Facebook and what may happen to the platform now.

Right down to paragraphing, punctuation and length of sentences, this social media post is very much in line with the type of language we find in formal writing.

Sure, not all social media posts are like this, and there are certainly ample instances of language play, misspellings, non-standard grammar use and slang in other platforms and posts. The point is that just like there is a continuum between speech and writing, there is also much variation in the language we find on social media and the internet. Online language is not homogeneous; it is not all impoverished and detrimental, nor does its existence spell the demise of language as we know it.

Like other genres of language, the crucial factor is context: what may be appropriate in one context, like using memes and emojis in a text message sent to a close friend, may not be appropriate in another, for instance, using these in academic essays.

In today's complex world, we are required to acquire all these norms. As our brains have clearly been coping with juggling both speech and writing for centuries, albeit with some effort and training, there is no reason to believe that social media will irreversibly destroy communication.

The potential of the human capacity to master just-in-time language production in different forms and guises, and to successfully navigate a constant flow of language in various modes, shows the task is not impossible. But it requires nuanced and sophisticated understanding to appreciate that what might be seen as a 'correct' or prestigious use (**standard form**) is no more important or crucial than a relaxed, colloquial in-group one (**non-standard form, regional form or slang**). Both are needed to maintain harmony in society because one is required for communicating across larger groups, perhaps the entire nation or beyond, and the other is needed for maintaining close bonds with local members of a close-knit social network (Chapters 4 and 9).

As I try to illustrate throughout this book, examples of exchanges from all channels of communication can help us understand language better, be they from speech, writing or social media. If language is indeed unique to us humans, the better we come to know the many facets and aspects of language, the better we get to know ourselves.

WANT MORE?

- Read David Crystal's (2007) introductory book on how language works.
- Check out Per Linell's (2019) updated discussion of the written language bias.
- Watch the Sign Language around the World (https://www.youtube.com/watch?v=MFleW3gVwII) video produced by *Attitude*.

2

MAKING UP WORDS

How many words do you know? It's impossible to tell, although later in this chapter, I discuss some ways we might estimate this number. However, before we can even begin to count, we need to know what a **word** is.

Talking about words invites a paradox. Most people have a sense of what words are. We have intuitions about words without being explicitly trained on how to identify them. For example, speakers of English know that *house*, *book, laughing, goodness* and *hangry* are all words, and *un* and *de* are not. Of all the ways in which we might break language down into units, say syllables, words, phrases, clauses, intonational units and so on, the word is surely the most recognisable one, the one we would be most comfortable working with.

Yet, when you delve deeper and look beneath the surface, or when you try to come up with a good definition of what a word is, even linguists begin to scratch their heads. It's complicated.

Should we count *laugh, laughed, laughing* as separate words when estimating someone's vocabulary? After all, they are very similar, yet not identical. What about *misclick*, is that a word? One way to check might be to look for it in a dictionary. The *Oxford English Dictionary* added *misclick* in March 2024, both as a phenomenon (**noun**) and as an action (**verb**), to describe the act of pressing an incorrect key. It is a pretty new word, but does it count? (Interestingly, my spell-checker has this word underlined as a misspelling at the time of writing.)

What about *mispost*? We have an idea of what it might mean (maybe to post something by mistake which you were not meaning

DOI: 10.4324/9781003621485-2

to), but it's not (yet?) in the dictionary. What if it were added later this month? And if we know what it means and can use it in a sentence so that everyone understands it, does that not make it a word just by its very use?

Instagram used to be a naming word (a noun), referring to a social media platform. Now it's an action as well (a verb): *just Instagram it* in other words, put it on Instagram, and also a kind of attribute (an **adjective**): *My bestie is so instagrammable,* meaning that she looks good in photographs (good enough to post on Instagram). None of these uses are (at the time of writing) in the dictionary. And that's just English, things get even more complicated when we begin to compare notes on words across languages.

All sorts of things get in the way of being able to define the concept of a word, such as the fact that languages are constantly changing and their lexicons are in flux. Added to that, languages have different structural elements which do not fit a neat and tidy definition of word-hood, for example, clitics, as I will exemplify shortly. And there is also the fact that there might be variation in how elements are treated within the same language, for instance, how they are spelled.

THE DIFFICULTY IN DEFINING WORDS

The simplest way in which we might define words is by thinking of written language and looking for spaces. Words are those elements that have spaces between them when written down. That seems straightforward (or is it straight forward or straight-forward?) until you realise that there is variation in spelling conventions. See (1) for some examples. Would we want to say that *apple pie* and *apple-pie* are two words or just one? How about *lipstick, lip-stick* and *lip stick*?

(1)

straightforward	straight-forward	straight forward
	apple-pie	apple pie
lipstick	lip-stick	lip stick
eyeliner	eye-liner	eye liner
motorbike	motor-bike	motor bike
pancake	pan-cake	

Incidentally, spoken language is no better at helping us identify words. It is tempting to think that there are pauses between words, a bit like spaces in written language. But as anyone who has tried learning another language in adulthood will know, word-segmentation is a great first obstacle for any learner. It is notoriously difficult to identify where one word ends and another one begins in a new language. Fluent speakers seem to just run words together without apparently taking a breath. It takes time for our ears to attune to new ways of combining sounds and to split language into chunks.

Another way to think of words is from the perspective of meaning. Putting aside their spelling differences, we can hopefully agree that all three spellings of *eyeliner* point to the same thing. So maybe that makes it one word. The main function of words is to designate concepts, to capture meaning. Sure, they need not only be concrete or easily describable concepts; they could involve complex and abstract concepts, but in one way or another, they designate something.

Instinctively, we tend to take the language we speak as a natural yardstick for how concepts might be organised into words. Yet there is nothing natural or logical about this organisation, and it happens to be completely arbitrary and language-specific. Consider the following sentences in English:

(2)

You all kiss.	You are all afraid.
They kiss.	They are afraid.
We kiss.	We are afraid.

When translated into Labu, a language spoken in Papua New Guinea, they become single words, as in (3) (Crowley et al., 1995, p. 272):

(3)

Monunu	Momolo
Sununu	Somolo
Lununu	Lomolo

While the English sentences have somewhere between two and four words each, Labu speakers only need one (single) word to express the same thing. How can this be?

Languages like Labu, Swahili and Turkish tend to glue several units of meaning together in a single word, each unit contributing a separate bit of meaning. In contrast, languages like English and French split these up into several separate words. In case you are curious, in Labu, the verb *kiss* is expressed by the form *-nunu* which cannot occur on its own (hence the hyphen at the beginning) and is always attached to the person doing it, for example, *se-, su-* or *so-* meaning 'they', *le-, lu-* or *lo-* meaning 'we', *mo-* meaning 'all' and so on. Similarly, *-molo* meaning '(to be) afraid' can not occur on its own.

A more extreme case of this kind of accumulation of units of meaning within words can be seen in a language like West Greenlandic (Fortescue, 2004, p. 1393):

(4) *nannu-n-niuti-kkuminar-to-rujussu-u-voq*
'It is really good for catching polar bears with (of a dog)'

As shown in (4), West Greenlandic has a single word, albeit a long and complex one, to express what English requires nine words for. By comparison, a language like Yoruba tends to have even fewer units of meaning inside each word (often only one), see (5). The point is that how the split is made varies with the language.

(5) *Nwọn ó maa gbà pọ́nùn mẹ́wǎ lọ́sọ̀ọ̀sẹ̀.*
'They will be getting £10 a week.'

We can arrange languages on a continuum between those that tend to have many different units of meaning (called **morphemes**) inside a word, like West Greenlandic, to those that have fewer units (but nevertheless some), like English, to those that have more words containing one single morpheme than words with multiple morphemes, like Vietnamese and Yoruba (Haspelmath & Sims, 2010, p. 4). This continuum comes with labels to designate key points along the way (Figure 2.1).

But here is another issue. What to do with contractions? Is *don't* one word or two? We can write the contraction in full to get *do* and *not*, and now we have two words, but do we want to consider *n't* a word? We cannot simply ignore it because it has both meaning and a form (it's a morpheme); clearly *don't* is different from *do*. Yet *don't*

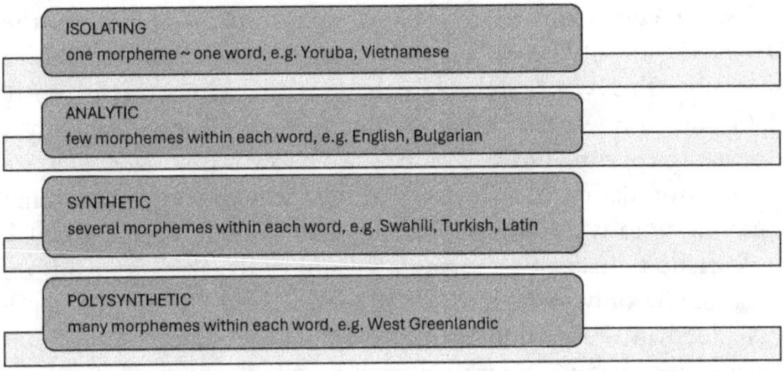

Figure 2.1 Language types according to their word formation processes

contains no spaces and *n't* never occurs on its own. It's both a word and not a word. Awkward.

The example of *don't* is not an isolated case. Come to think of it so is *it's*. Some languages have many examples of such forms, which lie somewhere in no-man's-land between words and non-words. Linguists term them **clitics,** and a great deal of research has grappled with how we should handle them. Here is an example from Romanian containing a sentence with three different clitics (clitics are given in bold):

(6)

*Nu-**mi** pasă dacă **ți**-ai găsit haina sau nu ia-**ți** măcar o căciulă.*
'I don't care if you found your jacket or not, at least take a hat.'

Earlier, we tried to think of words as being forms with a particular meaning and saw some problems with this view. Here is another problem: words are not the only elements in the language that have meanings. You might be surprised to learn that *un-* and *-er* have meanings in English, but I can assure you they do. In fact, you can even look them up in certain dictionaries.

When *un-* attaches to words like *tie, do, subscribe* or *twist* (verbs) they become *untie, undo, unsubscribe* and *untwist*, meaning 'do the reverse or the opposite action': *untwist* is to twist the opposite way, *unsubscribe* is to become no longer subscribed. Similarly, when *un-* attaches to characteristics (adjectives and **adverbs**) like *fashionable, friendly, intelligent, just*, the new forms mean the opposite ('not X').

I was recently surprised to find the word *unfriend* listed in the *Oxford English Dictionary* as being attested as far back as 1275. To my mind this was a relatively new word. However, its early 1275 meaning was that of an enemy, an *unfriend* was essentially a foe, that is a person, not an action, as we know it nowadays. Despite one citation dating back to 1659 of the term *un-friended*, meaning someone who is no longer a friend, its more common use today, to describe the act of removing a person from a list of friends on social media only came into use in the early 2000s, and this sense was added in the dictionary in 2013. This example demonstrates that old words can acquire new senses, which might make them seem like new words.

Just like *un-* attaches in predictable ways, so does *-er*. The morpheme *-er* takes verbs and changes them into nouns to refer to people who perform those actions, *write-writer, manage-manager, program-programmer, drink-drinker, drive-driver, buy-buyer, convene-convener*. There are exceptions as not every verb takes *-er* (*reach* does not turn into *reacher*, *pull* does not turn into *puller*), and not every verb follows quite the same predictable pattern of meaning. *Dresser* is not a person who dresses but a piece of furniture unless we are in a theatre play or talking about *cross-dressers*. *Cookers* are objects we find in a kitchen; we tend to use the same form (*cook*) for both the action and the person doing it (a process called **conversion**), though we also have the slightly fancier alternative: the French borrowing *chef*. *Bruiser* is not someone who bruises easily but quite the contrary, someone who is tough and aggressive. *Seem* does not turn into *seemer*, nor does *behave* turn into *behaver*.

Crucially, the power of *un-* and *-er* lie in the fact that although we do not think of them as words, our brains seem aware of their recurrent meanings and uses. If I were to invent a new word by reusing an existing one, like (*to*) *bag* and add *un-* to it, *unbag* would then have a predictable meaning, to take something out of a bag. I could even add *-er* to get *unbagger*, a person who takes things out of a bag. Our brains know a lot about language, but we do not realise what we know until someone else points it out.

These examples illustrate the incredible creative power that our brains leverage to both create and parse new words. While it may not be easy to articulate succinctly, in plain language what makes a word a word, we are certainly capable of enriching our lexicons with new examples. The constant waves of new additions entering dictionaries all over the world are testimony to this very fact. So, what are some of the main processes we use to create new words?

THE WORD MACHINE

New words do not come from thin air. As already hinted, languages reuse and recycle existing forms of words in various ways and obtain new meanings by a process of analogy. Sometimes we get new forms altogether, sometimes we add new senses to existing forms. Faced with a new word, we can trace how we got it by looking at its internal structure, but we cannot predict which new words are in the making, so we cannot be sure what the future will bring.

The strategy we have just seen with *un-* and *-er* in English and the Labu and West Greenlandic examples constitutes a common way of creating new words. This process, termed **affixation**, can be defined more formally as adding a morpheme, in this case, an **affix**, to an existing word, either at the beginning, the end, around it or inside it.

Prefixes like *un-* attach at the beginning of words and **suffixes** like *-er* attach at the end of words. English has many other prefixes and suffixes; see further examples in Table 2.1.

One difficulty in identifying prefixes and suffixes is that not all words containing the relevant string of letters in the right place are formed by affixation. *Restaurant* is not the product of *re* + *staurant* (*staurant* is not a word) and neither is *bistro* formed by adding the prefix *bi* to *stro*. Interestingly, *bistro* is borrowed from Parisian slang meaning 'little wineshop or restaurant' and its origin remains unknown (according to the *Online Etymology Dictionary*, the Russian-derived form *bee-stra* meaning 'quickly' is unlikely to be true). More investigation is sometimes required into the **etymology** (history) of the word before we can be sure of its internal structure.

Let's consider the examples of affixes in the table in more detail. You might observe that some affixes easily attach to just about every word in the language, whereas others are much fussier. Compare *-ette* with *-s* or *-ed*. They are all suffixes, yet it is harder to find words which take *-ette* compared to those that take *-s* and *-ed*. Most nouns, unless they are irregular can be turned into plural forms by adding *-s*. I should add that some verbs also take *-s* (to form the present tense for the third person singular, as in *John sings*), but that is a

Table 2.1 English prefixes and suffixes

Prefixes in English		*Suffixes in English*	
anti- (against X)	antisocial antibiotic anticlockwise anticrime	*-ment* (pertain to doing X)	government improvement accomplishment betterment
re- (do X again)	reread redo rephrase resurge	*-ed* (past of X)	talked walked stored loved
dis- (undo X)	disentangle disembark disappear distrust	*-s* (multiple collection of X)	books jobs affixes computers
bi- (two of X)	bifocal biannual bilabial bisexual	*-ette* (small version of X)	kitchenette towelette flannelette diskette

different *-s*. Similarly, many verbs take the *-ed* suffix to form the past tense form. Again, exceptions involve irregular verbs in some way, but even there, we find some regularity in certain irregular forms; *sleep* does not take *-ed* but becomes *slept*, very much like *weep* (*wept*), *sweep* (*swept*), *keep* (*kept*), *creep* (*crept*) – though *meet* does not become *mept* but rather *met*.

Put another way, some affixes are much more **productive** (attach easily to many words) than others. Furthermore, when these affixes attach to a word, they tend to preserve the word's grammatical category (see Chapter 3 for more on grammatical categories), which is to say that nouns that take *-s* remain nouns (*book-books, store-stores*) and verbs that take *-ed* remain verbs (*talk-talked, walk-walked, love-loved*). I am deliberately using the word 'tend' here because these are just tendencies and not without exceptions. Nevertheless, these characteristics have led **morphologists** (scholars who study word formation) to make a distinction between derivation and inflection.

Derivation is a process used to create new words precisely in the sense we might intuitively think of as brand-new words, that is, new forms, albeit related to an existing form, created by extending the meaning of the original word, and maybe even changing its grammatical category. A change in grammatical category is not always necessary; *social* is an adjective, and *antisocial* is still an adjective, no change there.

Not all words will allow this process, and it may depend on their meaning and sometimes their form. English *-ive* attaches to certain verbs, like *create* and *assert,* to make new words, *creative* and *assertive,* which describe a property (rather than an action). This time, there is a change in category, from verb to adjective. But we can equally think of verbs which do not take *-ive*, like *write, read, boil* and so on (there is no *writive*, *readive* or *boilive*).

In contrast, **inflection** is a pervasive process, whereby an existing form receives an affix that will not change its grammatical category and will bring with it a grammatical or functional and more abstract type of meaning, such as forming plurals, expressing the timing of events (past or future tense), expressing ownership (possessive) and other case marking, causative or passive forms and so on. Inflection is pervasive because it is highly productive, being relevant to a great majority of the words in the language (of the right category).

What is fascinating is that research on the world's languages has shown that overwhelmingly, languages favour suffixes for inflection processes. The exact roots and explanation for the **Suffixing Bias,** as this trend is called, are not entirely known (Polyanskaya et al., 2024). Whether cognitive pressures compel us to prefer adding material at the end of words rather than at the beginning, or whether there are other reasons driving this, we do not yet fully understand, but we do know that inflection tends to be overwhelmingly realised through suffixes.

On the topic of linguistic diversity, all possible affixation strategies are found in the world's languages, not just prefixation and suffixation. Some languages use **infixes**, which are affixes inserted in the middle of existing words, for instance, in languages like Tagalog, Sudanese, Pima, Oaxaca Chontal, Creek and Salinan. Although the presence of infixes is spread out geographically in languages all over the globe, overall, they are rare. Here are some examples from Tagalog and Sudanese (Moravcsik, 2000, pp. 545–546, the text between hyphens constitutes the infix):

(7)

Tagalog	*bilih*	'to buy'	*b-um-ilih*	'X buys/bought'
	gradwet	'to graduate'	*gr-um-adwet*	'graduates/graduated'
Sudanese	*budak*	'child'	*b-ar-udak*	'children'
	sare	'sleep'	*s-ar-are*	'sleeps'

It should also be added that in recent years, a debate has been raging between those who maintain the existence of infixes and those who claim that infixes are just prefixes or suffixes in disguise (led by Laura Kalin).

It has been claimed that English too has infixation, in taboo words like *not-bloody-likely*, *un-fucking-believable* and *abso-fucking-lutely*. However, not everyone agrees that these are really infixes. In the first example, the so-called infix does not interrupt an existing word because *notlikely* is not a word; it's two words. In the second and third examples, the infix is itself a free-standing word which complicates matters, although we are indeed dealing with a discontinuity in the form it's attached to (*absolutely* and *unbelievable* are indeed words, and they are 'interrupted' by the expletive).

A further type of discontinuous affix is the **circumfix**. Rather than interrupting the word to which it attaches, the discontinuity in a circumfix arises from an interruption of the affix itself. Put another way, a circumfix is an affix that attaches two parts in one go, a prefix-like element and a suffix-like element. Circumfixes occur in German, Dutch, Iranian, Samoan, Tagalog, Pashto and Uto-Aztecan. Like infixes, circumfixes are spread all over the globe, but overall, they are generally rare compared to prefixes and suffixes. Here are some examples from Afrikaans and Xhosa (Hendrikse & Mfusi, 2011, p. 43; the circumfixes are separated by hyphens).

(8)

Afrikaans ge- … -te	*ge-berg-te* 'mountain range' (*berg* 'mountain')
	ge-deel-te 'part' (*deel* 'divide')
	ge-dag-te 'thought' (*dag* 'think')
Xhosa e-…-i/eni	*e-ntab-eni* 'on the mountain' (*ntaba* 'mountain')
	e-umzi-ini 'at/in/from the homestead' (*umzi* 'homestead')

Does English have circumfixes? Yes, according to one scholar. The popular American animated cartoon *The Simpsons* set the motto of the town in which it is set, Springfield, as 'A noble spirit embiggens the smallest man'. Now the form *embiggens* is derived by adding *en/em+ ...+en* around the adjective *big* through circumfixation. This involves putting together two parts that do not occur on their own, but which come as a set. But is it productive? You bet! Aleš Klégr Praha (2018) conducted a search of natural language collections (corpora) and uncovered other similar cases: *enliven, embolden, enrichen, enbrighten, enfatten, endárken, enlargen*, among others. If you're looking at these words and scratching your head thinking you'd never use them, the point is that you could if you wanted to.

Before we leave affixation, it is time to dispel one of the most well-known language myths of all time. Deemed 'the Great Eskimo Hoax' by Geoffrey Pullum, this myth refers to the widely repeated but very much false claim that Inuit languages have many words for snow. Franz Boas, who studied Inuit languages, identified four words related to snow: *aput* 'snow on the ground', *qana* 'falling snow', *piqsirpoq* 'drifting snow' and *qimuqsuq* 'a snow drift'. His student Benjamin Whorf picked this up in an attempt to make a link between language and thought, suggesting that snow was so important to the Inuit speakers that they need much more than a single generic word for it, having instead a myriad of specialised terms to describe every possible type of snow they encountered. And in the process, four words became seven. It turns out that the four forms identified by Boas can give rise to many other words by attaching various affixes, but they are all related to the initial four; so, it all depends on how you define a word. In time, seven words for snow would become 50, and by the time the *New York Times* was done with Inuit, they had no less than 100 words for snow. Why let facts stand in the way of a good story? Come to think of it, how many words does English have for snow?

While most languages around the world enlist some kind of affixation to create new words, this is not the only mechanism for expanding the lexicon. A different word formation process involves reduplication. As the name suggests, **reduplication** repeats (or reduplicates) part of, or the entire, word to create a new word with a related meaning.

Reduplication is very common, though not in Indo-European languages, which perhaps explains why many people are unaware of it. As with other similar processes, it is found all over the globe. Here are some examples from Malagasy, spoken in Madagascar and Mangap-Mbula, a language of Papua New Guinea (Haspelmath & Sims, 2010, pp. 38–39):

(9)

Malagasy	*fotsy* 'white'	*fotsi-fotsy* 'whitish'
	maimbo 'stinky'	*maimbo-maimbo* 'somewhat stinky'
	hafa 'different'	*hafa-hafa* 'somewhat different'
Mangap-Mbula	*kuk* 'bark'	*kuk-uk* 'be barking'
	kel 'dig'	*kel-el* 'be digging'
	kan 'eat'	*kan-an* 'be eating'

A more controversial process is blending. **Blending** takes parts of words and mushes together into new forms: *brunch* is a mix of *breakfast* and *lunch*, *smog* a mix of *smoke* and *fog* and *glamping* is a mix of *glamorous* and *camping*. But is it really new?

Some argue that blending does not qualify as a true word formation process because the words arising from it are not really new words but recycled words, abbreviated and fused together. Words like *Twiple* (*Twitter* + *people*), *sexting* (*sexual* + *texting*), *Piloga* (*Pilates* + *Yoga*), *Tinderella* (*Tinder* + *Cinderella*) and *glitterati* (*glitter* + *literati*) all seem novel to me. Whether a true word formation process or not, blending sure is productive.

Apparently, the online dating application Tinder has its own dictionary of dating terms, many of the terms being either blends or abbreviations. Do we need such a dictionary? Maybe yes. Or maybe, as Germans might say, this will only *verschlimmbessern* the *situationship* (*situation* + *relationship*). (In case you are wondering, *verschlimmbessern* means 'to make something worse while intending to make it better', a blend of *verschlimmern* 'to make something worse' and *verbessern* 'to make something better'.)

Finally, let's consider compounding. **Compounds** are a bit like pyramid words. They are words that stand on the shoulders of other words. Take two flavours, *bitter* and *sweet*, and put them together: *bitter-sweet*; take two nouns, *motor* and *way* and put them together: *motorway*. Harder to see how we got *babysitting*, *kidnap* and *bluebottles*. Clearly not all compounds work in the same way.

While some compounds have a more democratic system whereby all the component words make equal contributions to the resulting new word, others have a hierarchy whereby one word is more important. This word is termed the **head**. The head specifies the overarching meaning of the new word and its grammatical category: *bedroom* is a kind of *room*, *gender gap* a kind of *gap*, *under side* is a kind of *side*, *parking meter* is a kind of *meter*, *watchmaker* is a kind of *maker*. The examples at the start of this chapter, in (1), are also compounds, and they similarly involve a head. Have you noticed a pattern? The head, where one is present, shows up on the right in English. But it need not be that way. In Māori, compound heads are on the left: a computer is *rorohiko* (*roro* 'brain' + *hiko* 'electric'), ink is *waimangu* (*wai* 'water' + *mangu* 'black'), calendar is *maramataka* (*marama* 'month' + *taka* 'revolve') and aeroplane is *wakarererangi* (*waka* 'canoe' + *rere* 'fly' + *rangi* 'sky') (Figure 2.2).

Given that compounds can be so different in different languages, what happens in the minds of bilingual speakers who speak, say, both English and Māori, when faced with a new compound they have not previously encountered? Is there an internal fight between potential heads? An ingenious and fun study has set out to test exactly that. See the next section for details.

Figure 2.2 Internal structure for the Māori compound *wakarererangi* 'aeroplane'

Illustration credit: Paul D. James

WORDING AND THE BRAIN

For various reasons, researching the bilingual brain is both exciting and highly challenging (see Chapter 7 for more on language in the brain). Working with Māori and English bilinguals in Aotearoa New Zealand, Alexander Onysko (2017) created novel compounds by pairing existing nouns in new combinations, such as *bucket philosopher, thought fridge*, and *canoe voice*. He then asked monolingual English speakers and Māori bilingual speakers as well as European (Pākehā) bilingual speakers what these words might mean.

The participants were shown 18 compounds which comprised a mix of the made-up forms alongside some common existing compounds. They were not told that some compounds were invented specifically for the experiment to ensure that participants tried their best to stay on task. The task was to provide as many meanings for each compound as possible.

The experiment showed that Māori bilingual speakers gave significantly more diverse meanings for the new compounds compared to all other groups (the monolingual speakers and the Pākehā bilinguals). For example, *voice canoe* was interpreted as meaning a canoe which you talk into, a canoe carrying a commentator in a boat race, but also as a voice that might be tough to understand, a flow of a person's voice, a telephone, or an earpiece device to assist hearing for the elderly. This greater flexibility in the choice of the head (*canoe voice* could be a type of *canoe* or a type of *voice*) shows the bilingual brain's versatility in interpreting meaning. Māori bilinguals seemed to be able to draw on both their languages, even when they were being addressed in only one. Several questions arise from this experiment, but one of the main takeaways is the astounding creativity and malleability of the human brain when faced with new words, and perhaps especially so in the case of bilinguals.

And speaking of brains, how do our brains deal with words in the first place? Do we store simple forms like *book*, *play* and *sure* in our heads and then derive them through rules anew each time to get *books*, *played* and *unsure*? Or do we also store some (or all) complex forms of each word?

For decades, word formation was understood as involving a kind of calculus with words and morphemes. Complex words were thought to be derived through rules and therefore not stored in the brain. Anything that could not be computed in this rule-like manner was memorised as a separate form; think irregular forms. The **mental lexicon** – the capacity of the human brain to handle words – is thus a kind of machine that balances out what is computed against what is stored.

This kind of approach was famously supported by evidence from (among others) ground-breaking early experiments like the **WUG test**. American psycholinguist Jean Gleason designed the WUG test in the 1950s (Berko (Gleason), 1958), as a clever tool to find out what children knew about language. It's not as if you could just walk up to a child and ask them. In order to appreciate the ingenuity of this experiment, first imagine showing a child a picture of a book and telling them *Here is a book* and then following this with a second picture, this time of two books. The child is then asked to complete the sentence *Now I have two* ____. Sure, you will get *books*, but why? Children might produce the predicted answer either because they had heard the word *books* before, in other words, by fishing it from memory, or by deriving it through morphology rules. Not a very useful experiment.

Instead, Gleason made up a nonsense word (**pseudo-word**) – the WUG – which she could be sure would be completely unfamiliar to her participants. She then taught children the word by showing them a picture of a wug: *This is a wug*. In the picture containing two of the same character, children repeatedly completed the sentence by adding the equally made-up plural *wugs*. Therefore, Gleason could confidently argue that they were computing (rather than recalling) the word.

The word-formation-as-calculus view found great support in formal theories of language, which saw it as an elegant and plausible explanation of how the human brain handles the lexicon. However, problems were soon uncovered with this view. If you think about it, a rule-based approach necessitates considerable cognitive heavy lifting. Memorising thousands of word forms might seem like a lot of work but consider deriving every single complex word through rules. A word like *discolourations* would require applying no less than four rules: take *colour*, add *dis-* to make a verb, then add *-ation* to make a noun, then add *-s* to make a plural noun. Do we really do that each time we use this word? No one has time for that in the bottleneck of just-in-time production (Chapter 1).

Further problems were uncovered by experiments showing that forms which might be expected to lead down the rule-highway did not produce the regular forms predicted. Several studies of past tense verbs reported that English speakers produced irregular forms rather than regular past tense ones. Let me explain. Participants were asked to produce past forms for (what might be perfectly regular) verbs like *search*, *seat* and *raise* and what they produced instead of *searched*, *seated* and *raised* were existing irregular verbs: the past tense of *search* was apparently *sought* (the irregular past tense of *seek*), *seat* led to *sat* (the irregular past tense of *sit*) and *raise* to *rose* (the irregular past tense of *rise*). None of these irregular past tense forms could show up unless they had previously been stored somewhere in memory in such a way that they circumvented the regular past tense rule. Experiments along similar lines from Dutch and Spanish corroborated the fact that not all that can be derived by rules actually is.

THE STRUCTURED LEXICON

One important factor in studying words and the mental lexicon is frequency of occurrence. Words are famously unevenly distributed across interactions: some words are used more often than others.

In general, a few words are used extremely frequently, while a great majority are used extremely infrequently. The most frequent word in English is probably *the*. The second-most frequent word, in a sufficiently large corpus, is the word *of*, which is used roughly half as much as the most frequent word. The third-most frequent word (*and*) is used a third as much as the most frequent word and so on. This is called a Zipfian distribution, after George Zipf, who first uncovered this law, as far back as the 1930s (Zipf, 1936).

Frequency effects influence how our brains store and deal with words. And how languages change. It turns out that irregular forms in any language are among the most frequently occurring words, as well as the most resistant to change. Take the irregular past tense forms of *go* (*went*) and *be* (*was/were*). These rank among the most frequently occurring past tense forms in the entire English language.

Scholars use **corpora** to extract frequency of use for different words and then group words into frequency bands. Unsurprisingly, such frequency bands can be helpful for estimating the total size of a speaker's vocabulary. The idea is that contrary to the layout of dictionaries, speakers do not learn words alphabetically. We do not have running lists of words, perfectly alphabetised in our heads, and no one would set out to read a dictionary from cover to cover as a form of entertainment. Unless they were perhaps a **lexicographer**.

Instead, we learn the most frequent words first because we encounter them first and use them most. As we learn more words, we expand our knowledge (often in predictable ways), dipping into more specific vocabularies and introducing more nuanced terms. With time, we welcome more sophisticated words into our repertoire, which are less frequently used by others. This is particularly true for people who attend higher education and whose vocabularies expand to include more and more jargon.

According to a team of researchers led by Marc Brysbaert (Brysbaert et al., 2016), the average 20-year-old American English speaker knows about 42,000 **lemmas** (simple words as you might find listed in a dictionary) and some 4,200 idiomatic expressions like *kick the bucket* and *down in the dumps*, derived from 11,000 word families (words together with their derived and inflected variants, for instance, *family, families, familiar, familiarity, unfamiliar* and so on constitute one **word family**).

But of course, there is no such thing as an average speaker, American or otherwise, and there is great variation between individuals. People with a university Bachelor's degree tend to know fewer words than those with a Master's qualification, who in turn will know fewer than those with a Doctorate. At the lower end, you can have people who only know about 27, 000 basic words (lemmas), at the higher end, as many as 52,000 lemmas. By the time this hypothesised average American English speaker reaches 60 years of age, they will have learnt another 6,000 extra lemmas, equivalent to one new basic word every two days.

This information is useful when testing someone's vocabulary because we can reverse engineer vocabulary tests with it. If we know the relative frequency of certain words, we can classify them into frequency bands, and knowledge of a word from one frequency band will likely imply knowledge of a word from a more commonly known frequency band. Instead of testing people on every word they know, if we pick our words carefully, frequency of use can help us gauge a good estimate fairly quickly. We can thus think of the lexicon as a structured list.

Frequency bands are only one way we might think of the lexicon as a structured list. Other ways to probe the structure of the lexicon involve examining relationships between words, for example, by looking at connections between words based on their meanings.

SYNONYMS, ANTONYMS, HYPONYMS AND OTHER -NYMS

According to the *Online Etymology Dictionary*, the word **semantics** comes from Greek *sēmasia* (signification, meaning), which is derived from *sēma*, meaning sign, mark, token, but also omen, portent, constellation, grave. These other meanings of the word are particularly relevant to how we organise words in our heads.

Imagine someone asked you what 'happy' means. One way to answer is by offering words with similar meanings, like *joyous, cheerful, content, merry, pleased* and so on. It would be unusual for the answer to be 'well happy is just the opposite of unhappy', not to mention rather unhelpful. 'Happy is the opposite of sad' might be more helpful but perhaps not the obvious way to answer the question, because **antonyms** (words with opposite meanings) are less easily accessible in our minds than **synonyms** (words with similar meanings).

However, experiments (Chaffin & Glass, 1990) have shown that there is another type of relationship that prompts us to react even faster than synonymy, namely, hyponymy. **Hyponyms** are words that instantiate a given category, best captured by expressions like 'X is a type of Y', where X is the **hyponym** and Y is the **superordinate** (category). A *diamond* (hyponym) is a type of *gem* (superordinate), a *Mercedes* (hyponym) is a type of *car* (superordinate) and *happy* (hyponym) is a type of *emotion* (superordinate).

In one experiment, speakers were shown statements of semantic relationships like *A car is an automobile* or *A condo is a dwelling* or *A plant is a vegetable*. These 'An A is a B' statements included either synonyms like *car/automobile*, hyponyms like *condo/dwelling* or false statements (*plant/dwelling*). Researchers recorded **reaction times** on the ratings, in other words how fast participants made judgements about these statements. These showed that participants were significantly faster at rating hyponyms than they were at rating synonyms (Chaffin & Glass, 1990).

In a follow-up study with Persian/English bilinguals, Farzad Sharifian (2002) discovered that speakers were faster at processing the relationship when they were presented with the superordinate word first, followed by the hyponym (*dwelling/condo*) rather than the other way around (*condo/dwelling*). Predictably, bilinguals were quicker to process word pairs in their first language than in their second, but the ordering effect (preference for superordinate word first) was observed in both languages.

These and other studies show that our brains organise lexical content in a relational manner; words do not hang in vacuum, but instead, they are linked to other words in a **network** or constellation. We understand and remember words in terms of how they relate to other existing words, and it is also existing words which help us to create and derive new forms, through a process of analogy.

WANT MORE?

- Read Martin Haspelmath and Andrea Sims' (2010) book *Understanding Morphology*.
- Laugh out loud reading Geoffrey Pullum's (1989) essay on the *Great Eskimo Hoax*.
- Watch Marcel Danesi's TEDEd talk on where new words come from (https://www.youtube.com/watch?v=Ytr28t5VzAs).

3

THE GRAMMAR HABIT

"Grammar is my favourite subject!" Now there's a sentence you are unlikely to hear. For one reason or another, grammar has managed to earn a terrible reputation. Grammar is also perhaps one of the most misunderstood areas of language study; it seems to mean different things to different people. Some people feel that being 'good at grammar' in English means knowing how to use the apostrophe in phrases like 'John's car' and 'the table's leg', or knowing the difference between 'their', 'they're' and 'there'. And many either see themselves as not being good at grammar (maybe because they get confused about these things) or as belonging to a minority (hence the meme: "My life is a constant battle between wanting to correct grammar and wanting to have friends"). But there is so much more to grammar than spelling and apostrophes!

One helpful way to think of **grammar** is as a set of language habits. Like other habits in our lives, they can be very useful, in the way that, say, brushing your teeth might be useful. Because habits are automatic, we don't have to constantly think anew every time we perform them, having repeated the pattern enough times that we are conditioned to it. In fact, we hardly notice doing it, and sometimes when we think too hard about it, we temporarily forget how to do it (a bit like remembering passwords). And like other habits, breaking them can lead to problems. Imagine the consequences of not brushing your teeth.

Though not all such cases can lead to problems, breaking certain grammar habits can also lead to some desirable effects. One could be that suddenly everyone is paying attention because something

DOI: 10.4324/9781003621485-3

unexpected has happened. For example, a common habit in English grammar is to have the **subject** (the main actor of a clause) first, followed by the **verb** (the action word) and finally the **object** (the bearer of consequences). We call this formula SVO. A regular sentence might be *Juliet loves Romeo*. This has the predictable subject (*Juliet*), verb (*loves*), object (*Romeo*) order. But I can break the habit and swap the order around: *Romeo, Juliet loves*. Now I have object, subject, verb. Is it wrong? Not necessarily. Not if I want to emphasise the fact that she just absolutely loves him (and then emphasise the word *loves* as I utter it) or that it is Romeo she loves, not someone else. I could make this more explicit by adding a contrast like: *Romeo, Juliet loves, Paris, she detests*. This kind of breaking-of-habit-for-effect makes the listener pay extra attention precisely because it presents an unexpected pattern that is not the default. I return to SVO order later.

More formally, we can define grammar or **syntax** (a commonly interchangeable term) as the system of recurrent patterns dictating how morphemes (Chapter 2) are organised into words, words into phrases, phrases into clauses and so on. In written language, it is also how clauses are organised into sentences, sentences into paragraphs and paragraphs into texts. Indeed, paragraphs and texts have internal structures too. In spoken language, we can identify recurrent patterns in how clauses are structured inside groups of clauses, and how these are organised in conversational turns. Such regularities make speech and writing easier to produce and decode because we know where to look for which elements.

Spelling is different from grammar, and the only time when the two overlap is when words that sound the same (**homophones**) have different meanings or grammatical functions, like in the meme *Grammar is the difference between know your shit and knowing you're shit*. The form *your* sounds the same as *you're* but the two mean different things. In grammatical terms, *your* is a possessive pronoun, expressing ownership, something you have, and *you're* is a contracted form of the subject personal **pronoun** *you* together with the shortened form of the verb *be*, which in this case is *are* (shortened to *'re*). And now that I have sucked out all comic relief from that meme, never to be laughed at again, hopefully it is clear that spelling lies at the heart of the humour and not grammatical structuring. Note also that if you say – rather than write – the meme, it is no longer funny. If the internet is to be believed, confusion between homophones, misplaced apostrophes and misused commas provides no end of comic relief. Once again, that is not really what the core business of grammar is about.

Instead, grammar is what stops an English-speaking passenger at an airport lost baggage claim in Istanbul (Turkey) from taking the English words *Where are my two suitcases?* and turning them into the literal *Nerede*(=where) *var*(=are) *beni*(=my) *iki*(=two) *bavullar*(=suitcases)*?* (Moravcsik, 2006). This seemingly Turkish sentence is anything but Turkish. In well-formed grammatical Turkish, our mishappen English passenger would have to say instead *Iki bavulim nerede?* ('Two suitcases-my where?'). Grammar is knowing that in Turkish, if you have a number word (**numeral**) like *iki*, you don't need to have a plural word next to it, like 'suitcases' because the *two* gives away we are talking about more than one item. Grammar is knowing that in Turkish, the question word (*nerede*) goes where the word it stands for might normally go, it fills the gap (in missing information).

Most of the grammar knowledge that we have comes from exposure to language, from speaking and listening. These acts allow our marvellous brains to soak up the abstract patterns and habits required to successfully communicate. In other words, much of the grammar in our heads is functional and unconscious. However, studying grammar and learning the words that describe recurrent patterns can help illuminate things that we knew all along, but which we did not know we knew, making explicit the knowledge that is buried in the back of our minds. It is also especially handy to do this if we are trying to learn another language, whose grammar is different from our own.

For language scholars, the field of grammar provides a way of documenting common structures in a particular language. This is crucial for various tasks, such as teaching the language to others or comparing its structures to those found in other languages, that is, looking for differences and similarities in grammar systems. The quest for consistent grammatical patterns that hold within most languages – it is very rare to find any that apply to *all* languages – is the holy grail of linguistics and has its own special term: **language universals**.

But if we can acquire grammar just from listening and speaking a language, why do so many of us feel insecure about our grammar?

And why are there so many books dedicated to teaching 'good grammar' in our bookshops?

GRAMMAR PATTERNS: AN EXAMPLE

Let's begin with an example. Imagine you're having a conversation and discussing a specific company. In grammar terms, the word *company* is something we call a **noun**, a type of naming word that typically denotes objects, people or places. *Suitcase* is a noun. So are *Romeo* and *Juliet*, and *happiness* and *love*. The former two are **proper nouns** (names of people, places or organisations), the latter two are **common nouns**.

Now, if you wanted to say something about the company, you could expand on your chosen word, first by clarifying that you are talking about a specific company (*the company*) and then by adding various bits of information, for instance, by adding a describing word (**adjective**), like *the American company* or *the greedy company*, or an entire **clause**, a chunk containing a verb and some other elements, like *the American company bought by TikTok*. Clauses that describe nouns are called **relative clauses**. There are different types of relative clauses you could add; see (1) for another example.

(1) This is the company that Bill Gates founded.

As with the previous example containing a relative clause, in (1), the noun *company* is followed by the relative clause (*that Bill Gates founded*). As far as the position of this clause goes, there is only one place for it in the sentence, and that is after the noun *company*. Putting it before the noun or at the start of the sentence leads to an **ungrammaticality**, like in (2) or (3), something that is not well-formed in English. The asterisk is a conventional symbol used in linguistics to point out ill-formed sequences.

(2) * This is that Bill Gates founded the company.
(3) * That Bill Gates founded this is the company.

While this ordering (noun + relative clause) might seem like common sense for English speakers, it is just the conventional pattern (a habit) that English speakers use for placing relative clauses. There is no reason why you can't have the relative clause before the noun. In fact, if you were speaking Basque, you would do it precisely that way around, and (2) would be grammatical while (1) would not. The same goes for Japanese.

Languages like Basque, Japanese, Korean and Turkish place relative clauses like *that Bill Gates founded* before the noun they describe (**modify**) and are called **prenominal** (*pre* meaning 'before'). Conversely, languages like English, Persian, Pashto and Icelandic, which place relative clauses after the noun they modify, are called **postnominal** (*post* meaning 'after'). Typologists, who document and compare structures found across many different languages, have convincingly shown that there are more postnominal languages than prenominal languages. The point is that there is no right or better way of ordering components; it just depends on the language at hand, which way around they are. This is what we call **cross-linguistic variation**, and common sense does not come into it.

Now let's return to our original sentence in (1). Compare examples (4)–(6). Which one(s) do you think is (are) grammatically correct?

(4) This is the company that Bill Gates founded.
(5) This is the company which Bill Gates founded.
(6) This is the company Bill Gates founded.

The answer is all of them. But that may not be what you have been taught at school. The difference between the three sentences comes down to the words *that*, *which* or simply nothing. In grammar, like in maths, 'nothing' can be meaningful, and we refer to it as **zero form**. You might have been taught that (4) is correct and that (5) is not. Why?

First, we need a bit more terminology. It's probably becoming apparent by now that grammar loves terminology. That's not because grammarians are trying to keep others from understanding what they are talking about but because it becomes rather long-winded to explain the same ideas and concepts repeatedly. Grammarians are busy people, you see. This kind of **jargon** is not unique to grammar or language; it is no different from talking about rugby, cooking or music.

Getting back to relative clauses, we can distinguish two main types: restrictive and non-restrictive. **Restrictive relative** clauses specify defining characteristics of the noun in question. For instance, in the earlier sentence *This is the company that Bill Gates founded*, the clause *that Bill Gates founded* is a restrictive clause because its role is to restrict the noun to one from a set of possible companies, namely the one Bill Gates founded. This property is one of its defining characteristics.

In contrast, **non-restrictive clauses** are simply used to give additional information, further (non-defining) details about the noun. An example might be the clause *which is based in New York* in the sentence *He founded a company which is based in New York*. It so happens that this company is in New York; there are many other companies based there also, so it narrows it down, but not in a defining way.

Grammatically speaking, restrictive relative clauses can be expressed by any of the forms above: *that*, *which* or zero. And yet, if you consult two of the most widely used English guides in Britain and America, namely, Henry Fowler's *Modern English Usage*, first published in 1926, and the *American Elements of Style* by Strunk and White, written in 1999, you will learn that the correct way of expressing restrictive relative clauses is by using *that* and not *which*. Both guides argue for a division of labour between *that* and *which*, so that defining (restrictive) characteristics are relegated to *that* and non-defining (non-restrictive) to *which*. No guidance is given for the zero form. The main takeaway from these guidebooks is that one should only use *which* in non-restrictive relative clauses.

Why should *that* be reserved for restrictive relatives and *which* for non-restrictive ones? In truth, for no real reason other than personal preference, stylistic convenience and a general view that giving each marker its own separate function makes for a neat and tidy system. The zero form is simply ignored. However, speakers certainly use it and quite often at that. In the past, the Microsoft Word grammar and spell-checker used to underline non-restrictive relative clauses containing *which*, but these days, it seems to have stopped.

It is important to pause here to ponder the difference between sentences like (2) and (3) on the one hand, and (4) and (5) on the other. While using an incorrect order in (2) and (3) leads to a lack of comprehension and understanding, using a stylistically dispreferred form may lead to an editorial raising of pens or eyebrows, but not to loss of meaning. These differences are important, as they highlight two important approaches to language: prescriptivism versus descriptivism.

THE GOOD AND THE ACCURATE: PRESCRIPTIVISM VERSUS DESCRIPTIVISM

Prescriptivism is a view of language characterised by an idealised, purist aspiration. Language **prescriptivists** tend to impose what they see as 'correct' or 'better' ways of writing (but sometimes also speaking) a particular language. Guided by personal aesthetic preferences for a particular style or by an ideological drive to standardise language conventions, prescriptivists attempt to teach the wider public the 'rules' of good writing to make language more uniform and to stamp out (what they see as) unwelcome variation.

In contrast to this view, many linguists subscribe to **descriptive** approaches to language. The **descriptive** school aims to describe how speakers use language, in all its forms and variants, neither evaluating them nor advising (prescribing) what should be used. This is not to say that linguists are not people with their own personal preferences, pedantic gripes and grumpy quibbles, but ideologically, descriptivists avoid imposing them on others in a directive way. This earns us great nicknames from the wider prescriptivist public, like professor-anything-goes (see David Crystal's 2005 book for amusing commentary on his personal experiences).

At times, proponents of descriptivism have vehemently ridiculed the self-professed superiority of prescriptivists as irrelevant, unhelpful and ignorant of language facts. For example, in 2009, Geoffrey Pullum wrote a punchy review of prescriptivist guidelines, entitled '50 Years of Stupid Grammar Advice'. It is a great quality of Geoffrey Pullum's to capture not just fascinating insights about language but also to lure readers with enticing titles. In this short essay, he pokes fun at those who provide prescriptive advice by lifting examples from their own writing that go against the very recommendations they are making.

Laughs aside, the effects of prescriptivism might be more wide-reaching than first thought. In a comprehensive article, Hinrichs et al. (2015) showed that prescriptive advice regarding restrictive relative clauses in English has indeed permeated their structure to such an extent that it has become a significant factor bringing about language change. Although there is no reason beyond prescriptivist advice for separating the functions and use of *that* and *which* in these clauses, when looking at modern English writing across time, it does seem that *which*-hunting is a real phenomenon shaping use. Writers of English really are paying attention to this advice, taking it seriously and adjusting their language accordingly (banning *which* from non-restrictive clauses).

Other notable examples of prescriptive rules include the prohibition of splitting infinitives and of preposition stranding. For brevity, I only discuss the first example here. The label **infinitive** is applied to a **verb**, which is a word denoting an action. Not all verbs are especially action-packed; for instance, *be*, *exist* and *sleep* are all verbs despite first impressions. Infinitive verbs are verbs that don't have overt marking signalling the timing of the action, which is to say they do not show **tense** (the grammatical word for timing). Most verbs in English have an infinitive form, and infinitives are easy to spot because they occur together with the preposition *to*. *To write*, *to know*, *to split* are all infinitives. Some verbs, modal verbs like *must* and *can*, do not have an infinitive form (we cannot say *to must* or *to can*). If I change the tense of the most important verb in the sentences below (the **main verb**), *like*, from say present (the time of writing) to past (prior to the time of writing), then the timing of the infinitive verbs changes along with it because it receives its tense from it, but its form stays the same.

(7) I like to write / to recognise / to split infinitive verbs.
(8) I liked to write / to recognise / to split infinitive verbs.

When prescriptivists caution against splitting infinitives, what they are essentially saying is this: do not insert other words between *to* and the verb, avoid sentences like *I like to often split infinitives,* where the word *often* splits the two words.

The source for this kind of guidance is Latin grammar. Latin structure prohibits split infinitives. But in Latin, this makes good sense because the infinitive form is a single word, there is no equivalent of *to* (the infinitive is marked by an affix in Latin). So, nineteenth-century prescriptivists decided it would be a good idea to apply the same rules in English grammar. Why? Because Latin was viewed as a prestigious language and why confine that prestige to Latin alone, when we could transfer some of it to English, albeit indirectly: this is how good my English is, it's practically Latin. This is of course a very silly reason and prohibiting split infinitives in

English makes no sense at all. Bill Bryson put it much better in his book *Mother Tongue* (1990, p. 137): "making English grammar conform to Latin rules is like asking people to play baseball using the rules of football".

Proponents of prescriptivism often cite concerns that language is deteriorating, that young people are no longer able to read or write 'properly', and that if we continue down this path of linguistic doom, all communication will be reduced to unintelligible, monosyllabic grunts. According to them, your average descriptive linguist, aka professor-anything-goes, values all forms and usages indiscriminately, too afraid to call out 'bad language'. However, this is a misrepresentation of descriptive linguistics. No one is saying that *This is that Bill Gates founded the company* is acceptable. We just want to be careful to not throw out perfectly intelligible and recurrent sentences like *This is the company which Bill Gates founded* for no other reason than someone's aesthetic sensibilities. Or to throw out perfectly grammatical sentences to follow the grammar rules of completely different languages just because these languages might be seen as prestigious. And what is more, as research has shown with restrictive relative clauses, the (erroneously) presumed young ignoramuses (or should it be ignorami? The *Merriam-Webster Dictionary* says either form is correct, but what would it have been in Latin?) of our time are apparently taking these guidelines rather seriously.

Let's now turn to a slightly different example, which has also attracted much bad press. Take the sentence *I don't speak no Latin.* This sentence contains two negative words, *don't* and *no*, hence its label **double negative**. If you ask an English teacher or editor, double negatives are not to be used in formal writing, such as academic essays or legal contracts. Some arguments against double negatives cite logic as a reason for this scorn: using two negative words in a sentence cannot lead to a negative interpretation because two negatives make a positive. However, in dialects like African American Vernacular English or Māori English, such use is perfectly valid and indeed a grammatical way of expressing negation. But we can look further afield. French speakers are told to employ two negatives when using formal French: *Je ne parle pas latin* (literally 'I no speak not Latin'), using both *ne* and *pas*. It is in colloquial spoken French that the single negative (just *pas*) is most commonly heard: *Je parle pas latin*. Italian also has double negatives: *Nessuno ha visto niente* (literally 'No one has seen nothing'), meaning 'no one has seen anything'. Finally, in a twist of sweet irony, once upon a time, colloquial Old Latin also had double negatives: *ne ningulus mederi queat* (literally 'not nobody to-heal she'), meaning 'she cannot heal anybody' (Greco, 2022).

Once again, variation in how languages build phrases, clauses and sentences shows that there are multiple ways of doing things, and one is not necessarily better than the other, they are just different. Although some speakers go on to attach evaluative meaning to certain forms, these arguments are not based on linguistic reasons but on social ideas and ideologies; low opinions of a certain group of speakers result in reverse-engineered low opinions of their way of speaking. This is a theme we will revisit in Chapter 9, when we consider language attitudes.

So far, we have seen that differences in grammar usage can arise not just between languages but also within the same language, across different dialects or varieties. What about other forms of variation which are not directly linked to a specific dialect; should it be *the committee are continuing to badger us with new directives*, or *the committee is continuing to badger us with new directives*? *You should pack those boxes*, or *you ought to pack those boxes*? *For whom* or *for who*? Well, it depends. Sometimes, there is variation within the same dialect because there might be an incoming change in the system and not all speakers have switched to the new form yet (as in the case of *whom* and *ought*). Sometimes, there is variation because speakers just cannot agree as to what they prefer (as in the case of collective nouns such as *committee,* which are singular for some, seen as a group of people, and plural for others, seen as multiple individuals).

There is no end to disagreements over grammaticality, and chances are, this state-of-affairs is here to stay. Whether we like it or not, borderline cases exist and speakers of different ages, ethnic backgrounds and different dialects will go on disagreeing with each other over the 'correct' form of a given phrase. The good news is that in the main, speakers tend to overlap in their intuitions about what makes a well-formed and intelligible sentence, so that communication can thankfully go on.

This is just as well, because a recent study published in the *Journal of Neurolinguistics* by Divjak et al. (2024) suggests that ungrammaticality is (literally) bad for our hearts. In their study, the researchers asked healthy British English adult speakers to listen to speech extracts containing sentences ranging between (uncontroversially) grammatical and (uncontroversially) ungrammatical forms. While participants listened to these examples, they were being monitored for physiological responses such as their heart rates and other similar symptoms. Researchers discovered that heart rates were statistically significantly affected by linguistic violations. In other words, hearing ungrammatical language is bad for your health. I would have liked to know the explicit knowledge of prescriptive grammar rules these participants had, but I don't think this was asked prior to the experiment.

WHAT YOU DON'T KNOW YOU KNOW: ANOTHER EXAMPLE

So high blood pressure and endless disagreements aside, what is grammar really good for? The point of having consistent structures in a language helps speakers (and writers) to quickly form clauses and sentences, while tending to the complex task of thinking about what they actually want to say. A system that contains sufficient predictability also helps listeners (and readers) understand what is being said and, at the same time, formulate their response. Grammar is one of the features (not bugs, contrary to popular belief) that helps ease the bottleneck-of-attention and enable just-in-time language production (see Chapter 1).

The great thing is that, all being well, grammar is the little helping hand that you never even see. Perhaps the most exciting type of grammar knowledge is the one you don't even know you have. Here is one such example. Recall the earlier phrases *greedy company* and *American company*. In my phrase of two words, the most important word (the **head**) is the noun *company* because that is the core thing discussed. Note that the order is adjective then noun. If I were speaking Polish, German, Czech, Hungarian or Gujarati, the order would be exactly the same. However, if I were speaking Breton, Welsh, Greek, Romanian, Somali or Hawaiian, then I would have to invert the order between the adjective and noun, to something like *company greedy* and *company American*, but of course with the correct local words.

Now imagine that we do not want to limit the discussion to just one adjective, and we want to string on many more adjectives, maybe four adjectives in a row. In English this might be something like *greedy, large, old, American company*. That is a mouthful, but it's nevertheless grammatical. Incidentally, some languages (Māori) cannot chain multiple adjectives together at all.

Even in languages where adjective chains are possible, they are rare, especially in spoken language, but when they do occur, there is a set preferred pattern which speakers like to follow. This pattern is more detailed than simply 'put the adjectives before the noun'. Studies of real language exchanges show that speakers consistently and rather unconsciously order adjectives like this:

size	→ condition	→ age	→ colour	→ origin	→NOUN
small, big	→ clean, dirty	→ old, new	→ blue, red	→ Irish, American	→ company

It does not mean that other orderings are not possible, but simply that other orders are just not the way we do things, not the right habit. Can you understand the phrase *greedy, old, American, large company*? Of course you can, you just did. But it takes longer to process it, that extra bit of strain and concentration to do so, and it sounds clumsy too. The reason for that is that you are not used to this ordering. We instinctively and intuitively adhere to the adjective order above because it is recurrent, making it efficient. No one teaches us to do it, we just know it and use it. And here is the best bit: so, does everyone else in the world. And speakers of Breton, Welsh, Greek, Somali and Hawaiian and others like them, who adhere to the noun then adjective order, use the same order, just in reverse.

At the start of this chapter, I mentioned the fact that many people report not being able to 'be good at grammar' because they feel overwhelmed or confused by the amount of jargon they might have heard around them, which seems opaque and complex. But the fact is that as proficient speakers of our various languages, we have implicit knowledge of the grammatical systems they have. From time to time, it is useful and interesting to dive under the surface and get to know the patterns more explicitly.

GROUPING WORDS INTO GRAMMATICAL CATEGORIES

There are other grammar things you know which you don't realise you know. One of these is the fact that we can group words based on how they are used in a clause. In some sense, we don't consciously think about this, but in another sense, this is familiar once we think about it. For example, earlier we saw different types of nouns: *company, Romeo, Juliet, happiness, love* and so on. We also saw different types of verbs: *speak, love, like, is, sleep* and adjectives: *greedy, old, large, American*. In many languages, words pattern neatly in categories like these. Here is how.

Let's start with nouns. Nouns share at least three important features. First, there are similarities in their broad meanings; they name things, people or places.

Secondly, they share similarities in terms of their position (or **distribution**) in the clause. In English, we can find nouns after adjectives; in other languages, like French, Irish or Gaelic, we might find them before adjectives. If the language has **articles** like *the* or *a* for distinguishing specific instances of the noun or any old example of it, we might find the noun after such words. But not always. Romanian has both types of articles, except that the **definite article** (*the*) is added as a suffix at the end of words (e.g. 'the boy' would be *băiatul*, using English words that would be *boy.the*), whereas the indefinite article is just like in English, a separate word before the noun (e.g. *un băiat* 'a boy').

Thirdly, nouns can change their shape in predictable ways. In English, many common nouns have a **singular** form (*book, company, box, life, place, noun*) and a **plural** one (*books, companies, boxes, lives, places, nouns*). As we saw in Chapter 2, the general rule in English is to add an *-s* at the end of the noun, but some nouns are what we call **irregular** and have an altered, though not completely random, form: *box/boxes, fox/foxes, enemy/enemies, life/lives, wife/wives*.

Other nouns have only plural forms: *scissors* and *trousers*. And you might think that just makes sense because these items always come in pairs. Why then do we have singular forms for *leg, hand* and *eye*? These matters have to do with something we might term countability. Some grammars distinguish between things you can count (**countable nouns**) and things you can't count (**mass nouns**), which are conceptualised as undifferentiated wholes.

Countable items have plural forms and occur with **numerals**, words like *two, three, four* and so on. In English (and many other languages), you can't say **two scissors* or **two pants*, you must say *two pairs of scissors* or *two pairs of pants*. Similarly, you can't say **two* *breads* or **two news*, because these are undifferentiated wholes and not to be counted. You can have *two loaves of bread*, and you might have *two pieces of news*. And you already know what I am going to say next. It need not be that way. This is just the convention or habit of English.

In Romanian, you can certainly have *două pâini* 'two breads' and there is nothing wrong with *două veşti* 'two news' because the nouns *pâine* 'bread' and *veste* 'news' (actually, *veste* has a singular form unlike English *news*) are countable, unlike in English where they are mass.

Most languages carve up the noun domain one way or another between count and mass, but they need not agree on precisely which nouns should go where. Interestingly, Yudja, a language spoken in Brazil, has only count nouns, and all its nouns can occur with numerals. I am not aware of any languages with only mass nouns.

Despite cross-linguistic differences, within individual languages, nouns share important characteristics, and the same is true for say, adjectives. They share a broad sense of meaning, specifying characteristics or features of nouns. We know where to look for them in a clause, in English, before a noun, in Greek, after a noun. We also know how they might change their shape. Typically they can be used in comparisons expressing the extent to which the quality applies: the **comparative** form (*safer, greedier, kinder, wider, smaller, taller, funnier*) or the **superlative** form (*safest, greediest, kindest, widest, smallest, tallest, funniest*). As discussed in Chapter 2, these forms are not always regular (*more intelligent*, not **intelligenter, most intelligent*, not **intelligentest*) or predictable (*good, better, best*). Moreover, some adjectives resist gradability altogether. What does it mean to be *more dead* or the *deadest*? But even though *dead* may not be the best example of an adjective, it's still classified as one, albeit somewhere at the periphery of the adjective sphere.

Verbs also form a neat category along these kinds of similarities: meaning, distribution and shape. So do **adverbs**, words that describe actions (verbs), like *quickly, speedily, hungrily, crazily*, but also *well* and *fast*. And to some extent, **prepositions** like *on, of, in, at, from* and *out of* in English. Other languages don't have prepositions (words which go before the noun) but have **postpositions**, which occur after nouns (hence *post-*). Postpositions are found in Estonian, Finnish, Basque, Korean, Japanese and Shuri. It might be surprising to learn that prepositions, despite being common in widely studied

European languages like English, French, German and Danish, may be typologically rarer across the globe than postpositions.

Now nouns, verbs, adjectives, adverbs and **adpositions** (pre/postpositions) constitute important building blocks for creating large chunks. We can form entire clauses with just phrases comprising these types of words. If we circle back to the start of this chapter and recall the first pattern we discussed, it was the order of the major constituents in English: S(ubject), then V(erb), then O(bject). This SVO order, I argued, is not immutable. We can play around with it for special effects or emphasis, but in general, English word order is relatively fixed. It won't surprise you to learn that not every language follows this SVO pattern. Once again, different languages do things differently.

Compare English with an example of a typical sentence in Japanese. If you don't speak Japanese, don't worry, it's still possible to understand what is going on with a bit more information. In order to compare larger structures between two languages, we need to consider not just the idiomatic translation of, say, the Japanese sentence in English, but also the function of each individual word or component in Japanese. Here is how cross-linguistic comparisons are provided in linguistics texts. The first line gives the original Japanese words, underneath you will find the word-for-word translation, and the third line provides the idiomatic equivalent sentence in English. This example is taken from Kuno (1973, p. 10), cited in the *World Atlas of Language Structures* (WALS, Dryer & Haspelmath, 2013).

(9)	*John*	*ga*	*tegami*	*o*	*yon-da.*
	John	subject	letter	object	read-past
	'John read the letter.'				

Ignoring other differences, let's focus on the order of major elements. How does the first line compare with the third one? In Japanese, the main actor (the subject *John*) goes first. This is like English. However, the verb goes last and in between these we find the object (*letter*). Unlike English, which is SVO, the default order in Japanese is SOV.

The three major components (S,V and O) can be organised in six possible orders: SVO, SOV, VSO, VOS, OSV, OVS. Astoundingly, all six order possibilities are attested, but they are not all equally distributed across languages. The rarest order is OSV. It is found in just four languages in the WALS sample, and these languages could hardly be more spread out over the globe. They are Kxoe (spoken in Africa throughout parts of Angola and Namibia), Nadëb (spoken in northern Brazil), Tobati (spoken in Papua New Guinea) and Wik Ngathana (an Australian Aboriginal language). But the most common order found is SVO (the Japanese order), found in over a thousand languages cited in WALS.

I hope to have convinced you that far from being a rigid and inflexible list of commandments, grammatical patterning is highly varied across the world's languages and is much better thought of as a set of flexible but useful habits, enlisted to facilitate communication. The diverse ways in which humans all over the globe structure their phrases and clauses are testimony to the enormous creative power of our brains.

WANT MORE?

- Read the grammar chapter in Kate Burridge and Tonya Stebbins' (2020) book *For the Love of Language*.
- Chuckle at Geoffrey Pullum's (2009) essay '50 Years of Stupid Grammar Advice'.
- Marvel at our linguistic diversity by playing around with the *Grambank* Database: https://grambank.clld.org/ (Skirgård et al., 2023).

4

LANGUAGE DAY TO DAY

What would you think if someone asked you, "Did you see that?" Specifically, what does *that* mean in this sentence? It depends, of course. It depends on where you were at the time and what you were doing or talking about, but it also depends on who is answering the question. Japanese-speaking children younger than ten answer this question (*Ima-no mita*?) very differently from (Japanese-speaking) adults, according to a 2025 study by Reiki Kishimoto and Kazuhide Hashiya.

Children are more likely to look for a literal answer and a more recent one too. For them, *that* is most likely right in front of them or at least within sight. For adults, on the other hand, *that* is more likely something unusual or exceptional and probably abstract too. Chances are that when talking to a child, the word will have them looking for a specific thing they can touch, a puppy, a toy, some object in the room. When talking to an adult, they will be thinking more conceptually about things that are out of the ordinary, like a recent news event or political development. The assumptions that children and adults make about what the speaker has in mind are simply different. And Japanese speakers are not unique in this regard.

This sentence illustrates the many ambiguities we navigate in our day-to-day interactions. We are constantly evaluating the context of interaction and making inferences about what might be meant, what is assumed and how to best respond. Words like *that*, *there*, *she* and *them* are flexible in their reference and thus allow us to provide different vantage points from which to present information. They are also not the only means for communicating what we want in just the right way.

DOI: 10.4324/9781003621485-4

Crafting our language for our intended purpose is not just a matter of choosing the right words, intonation and grammar, it's so much more than that. It is about fumbling with our words in indirect ways to show politeness or respect, it is about ordering the components in such a way to draw attention to the most important element while backgrounding less important information, it is about the implied and the deliberately vague.

DEIXIS: CONNECTING THE REAL WORLD AND THE LINGUISTIC REALM

Language does not capture an objective reality, a higher truth. It is simply one representation of the situation. As aptly coined by the French writer Anaïn Nin, "We see things not as they are but as we are". This more general truth equally applies to language. Most of what we encode in language relates to how we perceive (or want to portray), reality as we see it from our own perspective. We say things not as they are, but as we see them or want others to see them. Similarly, we decode what someone else is saying by interpreting their message from our own position.

But how do we connect language to real life? Let's consider the first few sentences from the novel *Lionness*, by Emily Perkins:

(1) Trevor turned off the alarm and rolled back to face me across the creamy hotel sheets. He gripped my wrist and held it on the pillow between us. 'I've got you.'

Although the characters of the story have not yet been introduced, these first few sentences immediately draw readers in with the promise of familiarity. They contain words like *me, he, my, it, us, I* and *you*. These words connect the narrative and hold it together like glue: *me* points to the 'speaker' (the narrator), *he* to Trevor, *my* back to the protagonist, *it* to the wrist, *us* to Trevor and the narrator and so on. It would be odd if *us* pointed to someone completely unfamiliar and previously not mentioned. We make these links instinctively, unquestionably.

These words, termed **pronouns** (words that stand in for nouns), are used to perform a similar job: they point to specific people or entities in the story. Through our own experience of what novels and stories are like, we understand that *me* points to the protagonist, the person telling the story. In contrast, *he* points back to Trevor, no world knowledge is needed to correctly identify the reference that *he* makes, it is built-in to how texts work. The noun *Trevor* acts as the **antecedent** of *he*.

In contrast, contextual information is needed to figure out that *us* points to the person telling the story and someone else (*us* involves two or more people), and given the previous mention of Trevor, that must be the someone else. And even more complex, the reference of *I* in the utterance *I've got you* can be successfully understood as *he* who grips the wrist, in other words *Trevor*, and *you* as the person whose wrist is being gripped, in other words the narrator. It is astounding to unpack just how hard readers work to figure all this out. Yet this feels effortless because we are so used to doing it.

Words like *I* and *you*, which require contextual information to be understood are termed **deictics** (Fillmore 1971). They are different from non-deictics, which are words that point to entities in the text in a mechanical fashion, without needing any world knowledge to interpret. Both types of reference (deictic and non-deictic) are not straightforward and require considerable cognitive work.

Because deictic words have inherently pointing functions, their meanings are variable and not fixed. Moreover, they can be used to point out various types of information, not just people.

Consider time expressions like *yesterday*, *today*, *tomorrow*, *next week*, *last week, this afternoon*. These words and phrases refer to different time periods depending on when they are uttered. For me, *next month* refers to May 2024. By the time you read this chapter, this will no longer be true for you, given the time lag between my writing a draft of the chapter and your reading of the published book.

Sending someone an email saying *See you in half an hour* could potentially lead to confusion if the meeting has not been prearranged because *half an hour* is likely to be written and read at different times, thereby pointing to different points in time.

Monday week presents another possible confusion if uttered on a Monday. For some people that could mean the following Monday, for others two Mondays later. It's probably made increasingly more confusing because of its rarity, leading to uncertainty in how it's meant to be used in the first place.

English has three temporal words capturing the sequence of days: *yesterday*, *today* and *tomorrow*. There is also *the day after tomorrow* but that is a longer expression and not a single word. There are other languages with this kind of system, to mention just one example: the Australian language Diyari *waldawirti* 'yesterday', *karrari* 'today', *thangkuparna* 'tomorrow'.

Arabic has a more elaborate system, containing five distinctions: *albarahati* 'day before yesterday', *albaraha* 'yesterday', *alioum* 'today', *ghuden* 'tomorrow', *badaghuden* 'day after tomorrow'. Romanian makes similar distinctions. So do Chinese, German and Punjabi.

There seems to be a nice symmetry in having systems where the current day is then surrounded by labels for the previous and following day, and in some cases, by labels for two days prior and two days following today. Maybe there are no systems with an even number of labels. If you go forward in time, you want to perhaps go backward in time by the same number of days? Wrong. Spanish has (not three or five but) precisely four distinctions: *anteayer* 'day before yesterday', *ayer* 'yesterday', *hoy* 'today', *mañana* 'tomorrow'. No day-after-tomorrow word in Spanish.

According to Yan Huang (2013), the most elaborate system is found in languages like Greek, which have a seven-distinction nomenclature: *antiprochthes* 'two days before yesterday', *prochthes* 'day before yesterday', *chthes* 'yesterday', *sinera* 'today', *avrio* 'tomorrow', *methavrio* 'day after tomorrow', *antimentha* 'two days after tomorrow'. That's the entire week expressed without weekday words at all!

As these examples illustrate, the exact way in which languages split up time is conventional and arbitrary. The expressions used help to connect actual events in the real world with the ways in which we talk about them.

Place deixis is just as fascinating as **temporal deixis**. Here too, we find variation in how different languages carve up space. For example, we could describe the location of an entity in relation to certain **intrinsic** properties, like *on the side of the house* or *at the foot of the mountain*.

Another system relies on **relative** positioning, like *to the left of the table* or *the right of the house*. English has words like *here* and *there*, which act as **egocentric** markers, markers that locate entities based on the speaker's position: locating them as being close-to the-speaker (*here, this*) or far/further away from the speaker (*there, that*).

Middle English had a third term, *yonder*, meaning away from both speaker and hearer, but somewhere along history, this distinction was dropped in standard English and only remained in certain dialects. Of course, close-to-the-speaker is relative to who the speaker is (it changes when someone else is speaking), and what we are talking about. Saying *here in this house* refers to a different position than *here on this planet*; these expressions encapsulate different orders of magnitude in how we perceive the space in question. There are many other languages with a three-tier system, including Arabic, Breton, Chinese, Palauan, Portuguese, Spanish, Tagalog, Turkish and Welsh.

Dyirbal has four distinct terms. According to Australian linguist Bob Dixon (2022, chapter 13), the Dyirbal terms do not match English ones all that well, but to give an idea of the system, there is one form that roughly translates to 'here, near the speaker and probably visible' (*ya(la)-*), one which means 'there, visible but not near the speaker' (*ba(la)-*), one meaning 'not visible, far distant' (*ŋa(la)-*) and a fourth which is quite indefinite, referring to 'a non-specific somewhere' (*wuñja-*). There are languages with even more distinctions; Malagasy has six distinctions, Koasati has seven; Inuktitut languages are reported to have 686 different forms (Huang, 2013, p. 193). It is hard to imagine anyone needing 686 different spatial forms, and suddenly the words for snow myth springs back to mind.

A third type of system for encoding spatial relationships involves **absolute** positioning. These distinctions are more precise, expressing location in terms of specific landmarks or cardinal directions, and sometimes a combination of the two: *downriver, north of the mountain* or *east of the table*. Many Australian Aboriginal languages, like Pormpuraaw and Guugu Yimithirr, work this way. Speakers of these languages need to constantly stay oriented in cardinal space to be able to speak their languages and to conduct even the most mundane of interactions, like asking: 'Can you please move your leg a bit north-north-east?' (uttered with Pormpuraaw or Guugu Yimithirr words).

These distinctions raise questions about what it means for our brains to be able to speak different languages. Do we really see the world and reality differently, depending on whether we think of space in absolute versus relative terms? And how do these distinctions manifest themselves in bilingual brains?

INFORMATION PACKAGING

Most interactions tend to involve groups of words rather than single words. Crucially, how we group words makes a difference to how the message will be received. One such difference relates to what the listener will perceive as being the most salient part of the message. Compare the following sentences:

(2) The Prime Minister went to London by train.
(3) It was by train that the Prime Minister went to London.
(4) How the Prime Minister went to London was by train.
(5) London was where the Prime Minister went by train.

In essence, they mean the same thing. Yet there are differences between them. What is the first sentence really telling us about? Depending on where the main stress is placed, it could be telling us about the destination of travel (if *to London* is stressed), the mode of transport used (if *by train* is stressed) or about the person undertaking the journey (if *The Prime Minister* is stressed).

In spoken language, we can use our voice to direct attention to the newsworthy information by increasing the loudness or length of the word (or syllable) that is most important. In writing, we could use italics or bold font to indicate the point of emphasis.

But there are other ways to highlight newsworthy information. The sentences given in (3)–(5) are examples of **clefts**. These are special grammatical tools used to highlight what matters most in the message. Because English has a relatively strict word order (Chapter 3), clefts are useful formulae that allow speakers to change the ordering of words without going against English rules. Clefts come in different flavours, depending on the elements used to construct them; for instance, English has it-clefts, wh-clefts, reversed wh-clefts, since-clefts, all-clefts and so on. The names are not important, but the point is that they are all put together in a similar way, for a similar purpose. Here is how.

First, take a regular sentence (sometimes called an **unmarked** sentence) like that in (2), then extract the most important element from it; it might be *to London*, it might be *by train*. This element is then placed in the position of highest prominence in the cleft formula, either at the end or at the beginning, depending on cleft type. It is thus that (2) transforms into (3), an it-cleft, which brings forward *the train* (not a subject but an object in the original unmarked sentence). Or (2) could be changed to (4), a wh-cleft that shifts *the train* right to the end of the sentence. The first and last positions in a sentence are deemed to be most important because we are busy people with limited attention spans, and we often remember that which comes first or last, forgetting the bits in the middle.

The function of clefts is therefore to place in focus the element which is deemed of highest importance. Although English is rich in cleft types, it's not unique in having them, despite being the language that got to name the various types of clefts. French also has clefts, as do Latin, Italian, Spanish and other Indo-European languages. Here is a cleft from German (De Cesare, 2014, p. 18):

(6) *Es war das erste Mal, dass er öffentlich in Erscheinung trat.*
'It was the first time that he made a public appearance.'

Another strategy for highlighting newsworthy information involves the use of special particles that attach to or near the relevant elements that we want to bring to attention. These **focus markers** are found in many languages, including Japanese, Korean and Hungarian. Some languages use affixes (Chapter 2), which attach to existing words to mark prominence, others use (free-standing) words.

Perhaps the most intuitive strategy involves simply playing around with (regular) word order to signal special emphasis. As mentioned earlier, the first and last things we hear tend to be most memorable. Languages vary in this aspect too, even within the same language. In spoken Russian, the first position is most important; in written Russian, it is the last (Miller & Weinert, 1998, p. 190). The first element often coincides with the topic of a sentence too, and depending on the language, it also coincides with the subject. It quickly gets complicated, but it suffices to say that in languages with more flexible word order, elements can move around to positions of prominence more easily, as we find in German, Hungarian, Russian, Polish and many Romance languages. Here is an example from spoken Italian (Brunetti et al., 2011, p. 312):

(7) *Pure la LINGUACCIA,* *gli* *fa,* *la rana.*
even the tongue to-him he-puts-out the frog
'Even the tongue did the frog put out to him.'

In an otherwise typical word order version of the sentence above, we would find the phrase *pure la linguaccia* 'even the tongue' occurring after the verb *fa* 'he-puts-out' (in Italian, the verb changes with each person so the pronoun becomes redundant and is often left out; a phenomenon called **pro-drop**). However, as indicated by Brunetti and her team, the version given in (7) is perfectly grammatical but **marked** in the sense that the unusual order highlights the important fact that even the tongue was put out. The use of capital letters also indicates special stress.

English only allows a limited amount of such movement, typically for contrastive purposes, see (8) and (9). It is used sparingly, and overuse causes irritation.

(8) Wine, I like, beer I don't.
(9) Not those old repeats again, I want to see the new series.

Sometimes, the highlighted element can move right out of the sentence altogether, leaving a gap which is filled with a corresponding pronoun, as in (10) and (11) from French. This strategy is frequent in French, so it has its own special label: **left dislocation**. Left dislocation is also possible in English, but as with other word order movements, it is rare.

(10) *Moi, je suis très contente de rester à la maison.*
'[As for] Me, I am very happy to stay at home.'
(11) *Le lion, il court autour de la cage.*
'The lion, he is running around the cage.'

These examples illustrate just how much effort and linguistic energy speakers and writers put into communication. They sometimes play around with the structures in their language and with the ordering of components so that their message is not just understood but also appropriately interpreted, directing their interlocutor's attention just where they want it.

If you've been looking at job ads recently, you might be aware that practically all of these include a need for applicants with excellent communication skills. Communication ability is an extremely sought-after skill; no one ever seems to want to settle for average communicators. But what does good communication look like? Very few of us can really say. This very question inspired and probably tormented one of the most influential language philosophers of all time: Paul Grice.

GRICEAN MAXIMS AND THE COOPERATIVE PRINCIPLE

Today, Paul Grice is known as the man behind (arguably) the most comprehensive theory of conversation. Despite his sharp mind and reasoning, or perhaps because of these very qualities, Paul Grice did not commit his landmark theory to print until the end of his life. But his ideas have stood the test of time and continue to influence our thinking today, as they are being applied to new data and contexts of communication, more recently to online language and conversational chatbots.

Grice saw human communication as a process in which conversational partners enter an unspoken contract, with everyone buying into a particular way of doing things. In the same way that drivers get into their cars and take it for granted that all other drivers will obey the road-code and follow the rules for driving of the country they are in, like driving on the same side of the road, stopping at red lights and so on, conversational partners assume that their interlocutors are coming to the interaction with the intent and willingness of grasping what is being said, to the best of their ability and in good faith. Jumping into a car without that assumption would be an extremely scary prospect. Even though we know that sometimes people don't signal when they should and run red lights too, in general, all being well, our expectations are that most drivers are reasonably cooperative. The same thinking goes for conversation. Hopefully, most of the time, our listeners are not there to twist our words and deliberately misinterpret what we say.

Like a road-code for conversation, the **Cooperative Principle** formulated by Grice invites speakers to: "Make your conversational contribution such as is required, at the stage at which it occurs, by the accepted purpose or direction of the talk exchange in which you are engaged" (Grice, 1989, p. 26).

This overarching principle gave rise to nine more detailed and specific Maxims, which Grice organised into four main types, nowadays termed **Gricean Maxims** (of Conversation), see Table 4.1.

Like a modern-day self-help guide, Grice is addressing real speakers in his theory, guiding them towards a better communicative experience.

It is immediately striking that one of the maxims – the Maxim of Relation – is a lot less specific than the other three. Perhaps it is no coincidence that an entire theory of discourse bearing its name, *Relevance Theory*, was put forward by Dan Sperber and Deirdre Wilson, who drew inspiration from Paul Grice's Maxims. They must have taken one look at this Maxim and thought to themselves that this is just not sufficient, more needs to be said there (maybe they thought Grice was himself not following his Maxim of Quantity, a shortcoming they set out to fix).

The Maxims go a long way towards explaining what makes for a successful interaction, and how we go about making sense of what others say. More often than we realise, speakers are indeed following

Table 4.1 Gricean Maxims

Maxim of Quantity	(i) Make your contribution as informative as is required (for the current purposes of the exchange). (ii) Do not make your contribution more informative than is required.
Maxim of Quality	Try to make your contribution one that is true. (i) Do not say what you believe is false. (ii) Do not say that for which you lack adequate evidence.
Maxim of Manner	Be perspicuous. (i) Avoid obscurity of expression. (ii) Avoid ambiguity. (iii) Be brief (avoid unnecessary prolixity). (iv) Be orderly.
Maxim of Relation	Be relevant.

Source: Summarised by Huang (2013, p. 25).

the Maxims even when they appear to not be doing so. Let's look at a much-cited example in this field:

(12) Wife to husband: I am leaving you.
Husband's response: Who is he?

This pair of utterances only makes sense if you know enough about romantic relationships, conventional matrimonial commitments and the precarious position that women have enjoyed in hegemonic societies for centuries (whereby being alone is less preferred than being in a relationship). The assumption made by the husband – but which remains unspoken – is that the wife has found another partner and is intending to be with him instead, that being the obvious reason for her leaving her husband ('leaving' is taken to mean that she intends to end the relationship).

AI tools are already sufficiently sophisticated to make correct inferences and produce this interpretation. However, a young child with limited understanding of romantic relationships will struggle to follow what's going on. Context and world knowledge are hugely important.

The implication that remains unspoken in this interaction (that there is another man in the woman's life) can only be arrived at if we take the Gricean Maxims for granted and despite the evidence – which initially suggests the response is not relevant – we keep inferring until a reasonable explanation presents itself. Even when a Maxim appears to be violated (in jargon terms, **maxim flouting** or **maxim exploitation**), listeners persist in their deduction towards finding a plausible explanation and a fitting interpretation. All this is done subconsciously; most of the time, we don't even know we are doing it.

When Bill Clinton made the 1998 public statement: *I did not have sexual relations with that woman*, he was arguably flouting the Maxim of Quality. Whether he was telling the truth or lying depends on how we understand the meaning of the phrase *sexual relations*. If he had uttered *To the best of my recollection, I did not have sexual relations with that woman*, that would qualify as an opt-out of the Maxim; a disclaimer casting doubt on the quality of the statement made (*maybe I just don't remember correctly*).

While Gricean Maxims outline general principles for successful human (to human) communication, they can also be used as a useful benchmark to evaluate human-to-machine interactions, such as interactions between humans and chatbots.

As our modern world is changing, many of us are finding ourselves 'in conversation' with machines. Whether we are ordering a taxi or a pizza, or asking for directions, it is not unusual to interact with automated assistants. These are essentially computer programs designed to assist us in various ways, and many corporations are competing to create the best system. Such virtual assistants are sometimes called conversational agents but increasingly, they have **anthropomorphic** names, like Siri, Claude, Watson and Alexa, designed to mimic a human-to-human experience by leading us to think we are talking with another person (see Chapter 8 for a more in-depth treatment of computational tools).

Because we are more used to speaking with humans than with machines (at least for now), figuring out what makes the best system means comparing it to what we think of as 'normal' conversations (see also the Turing Test, Chapter 8). Companies employing AI assistants want to ensure that customers have positive experiences while interacting with these assistants, in other words, that they are not going to get confused, frustrated or annoyed while interacting with them. I recently witnessed my children interacting with Siri, and it struck me just how persistently polite this chatbot was being. This exaggerated politeness does not seem to me to be mimicking normal conversation. But it's not easy to figure out how to gauge the pragmatic competence of chatbots, and this is precisely where Gricean Maxims come into play.

Scanning recordings and transcripts of interactions between humans and AI assistants indicates that adherence to the Gricean Maxims is likely to lead to higher (human) engagement and to faster reaction times. **Reaction times** capture how quickly each party is able to respond, so faster times correlate with quicker responses and increased ability to make sense of what is being said. This matters especially if you are a company trying to maximise user experience and profits.

Moreover, some Maxims seemed to be more important than others. Violating the Maxim of Relevance was particularly damaging for communication. Additionally, the Maxim of Quantity was also deemed highly important. Interestingly, the Maxim of Quantity was especially noted in respect to building trust between humans and chatbots. For example, in one study (Jacquet et al., 2019), humans reported that when a virtual assistant repeated part of their query in their answer, they felt reassured that their question was interpreted correctly. I guess that for now, many of us still have reservations about chatbots and their ability to 'understand' what we want from them, so building trust is an important dimension in human-to-machine interactions.

Somewhat puzzlingly, the impact of violating different Maxims seemed to slow down response times for male speakers more than for female speakers. Why should this be? We don't really know; various explanations are being considered, but the jury is still out on this one (see Chapter 5 for a discussion of language and gender).

WHAT YOU SAY, WHAT YOU INTEND AND WHAT THEY HEAR

That being said, there is more to successful communication than following Gricean Maxims. Speakers and their interlocutors come to the conversational table with certain expectations that go beyond the Maxims. When these expectations are not met, they can be confused, annoyed or … simply entertained. Consider the following meme:

(13) Did you know on the Canary Islands there is not one canary?
And on the Virgin Islands?
Same thing – not one canary there either!

This is funny because the expectation raised by the structure of the first sentence fails to materialise in the second sentence: the negated element is not given within the sentence itself (there is no virgin there either) but is the same as the negated element in the first sentence (there is no canary). Example (14) says essentially the same thing but the way it expresses the message kills the joke. This is because the way information is presented is crucial for guiding hearers in how to make sense of the message.

(14) There are no canaries on Canary Islands.
And there are no canaries on the Virgin Islands.

Often, the packaging of information will have drastic consequences for its interpretation. Let's consider another example. Despite best intentions, even innocent-seeming well-wishes can backfire if phrased in unexpected ways: *Have a nice day!* sounds friendly but its near synonymous counterpart: *Enjoy the next 24h!* is ominous (the example comes from the *Language Nerds*).

As proficient members of a language community, we are socialised to recognise not just correct pronunciation, spelling and grammar but also conventional ways in which language is used to get things done. We communicate with one another for a myriad of reasons, not just for transferring information, but also to flirt, compliment, promise, deceive, insult and threaten. These goals are associated with linguistically and culturally specific scripts, termed **speech acts**.

It may sound dramatic but speaking is not just a passive event; certain types of speech can irrevocably change life as we know it. For instance, the act of *pronouncing someone husband and wife* (a speech act labelled a **performative**) changes the marital status and possibly the name of the said individuals, depending on their culture and preference. Promising to tell *the truth, the whole truth and nothing but the truth* in a court of law can land the speaker in jail for perjury if caught lying, again depending on the country and its laws. Thankfully, not all statements have such dire consequences. This observation led philosopher John Austin (1975) to distinguish between performatives (as above) and **constatives**, sentences that present facts or states of affairs and which can be said to be either true or false.

Like Grice, Austin also thought long and hard about what happens during interactions. When a message is communicated, several things take place at the same time. One is that the speaker expresses the message by putting it into words (**locutionary act**). A second is that the speaker has a specific intention or purpose that they want to communicate to their listener (**illocutionary act**). Thirdly, the listener takes away a message or interpretation from this interaction (**perlocutionary act**).

Let's consider an example. If I were in France and uttered *Je parle pas bien le français, ma langue maternelle est l'anglais.* 'I don't speak French well, my mother tongue is English.' to a new acquaintance, the locutionary act involves me finding the correct French words to formulate my statement and uttering them. The illocutionary act is my intention to have them speak to me in English and the perlocutionary act might be that they reply in English (assuming they were able to). In an ideal world, there will be a perfect alignment among these three acts, but that is not always the case. What we say and how we say it may end up having a different effect on the listener than the one we intended. Teasing apart these aspects of communication can help us better understand how to get it right and what happens when we don't. If my aforementioned interlocutor was being facetious, they might choose to ignore my indirect request and keep chatting away in French.

Of course, the beauty of the language is that there's always another way of saying the same thing. In this case, a completely different locutionary act might look like the meme below, based on Quentin Tarantino's 2014 movie *Pulp Fiction* (notice the word order change here, leading to a left dislocation structure). Using this locutionary act in the situation above will clearly not lead to a successful interaction (Figure 4.1).

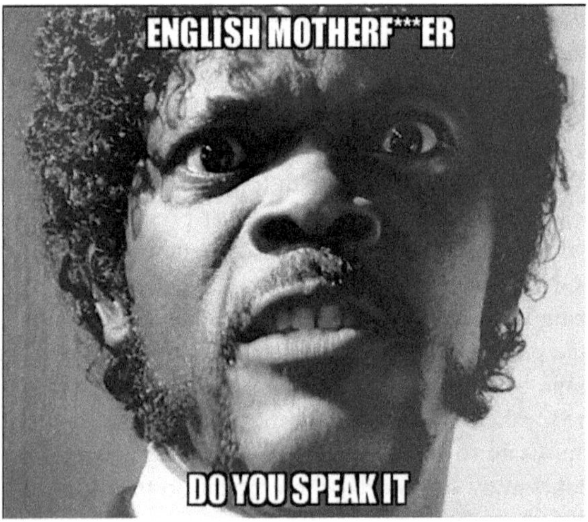

Figure 4.1 English MF – Do you speak it?

Source: Know your Meme. https://knowyourmeme.com/memes/english-motherfucker-do-you-speak-it

Let's consider another example. During the Covid-19 pandemic, many governments, organisations and individuals took to social media advising others to *Take care* and *Stay safe*. Now on the face of it, this appears to be a positive and kind gesture, but is it always so? In a study that Jessie Burnette and I conducted (Burnette & Calude, 2022), we analysed hundreds of Twitter posts from 2020 to 2021 relating to Covid-19, which contained phrases like *stay safe*. Here is an example from our data:

(15) Back into lockdown we go… Whanau ['family'] when you are told to stay home and isolate you STAY HOME. play your part!!!. Everyone stay safe this isn't a joke #COVID19nz #COVID #aotearoa #newzealand #jacindaardern #isolation #lockdown #auckland

Is *stay safe* kind here? We thought not. Given the text surrounding it: *STAY HOME* and *play your part!!!* and *this isn't a joke*, the phrase is at best pointed advice, at worse a threat: if you don't stay home, you won't be safe and neither will others. The well-wisher is really a directive-giver. What is happening here and how do we know to interpret (15) as a threat or command? In order to unpack these differences, we need to consider linguistic politeness.

POLITENESS AND IMPOLITENESS

Harmony is indisputably a desirable outcome in any society. However, there are other desires that people have besides societal harmony, and some impinge on it. One of these is the need to be liked and appreciated. Another is to be autonomous and independent, to be able to freely go about daily activities without being constrained. While we try to achieve these things, our efforts sometimes impinge on other people, who are themselves pursuing their own similar needs.

One example of a speech act that conflicts with the needs of others is the **directive**. Directives are commands, warnings, advice or threats. Telling someone to do something, even helpful advice, can come as a constraint on their ability to do as they please. The Twitter post in (15) is a directive. Yet there are situations in which we do want to provide this kind of advice without offending anyone.

In their theory of linguistic politeness, Stephen Levinson and Penelope Brown (1987) talked about the concept of a person's **face**, a concept which they borrowed from Goffman to name the various desires that individuals have. If a speaker is about to utter a threat to a person's face, several options present themselves: to go ahead and commit the (face-threatening) act or to mitigate it with some politeness markers of various types. In the first instance, speakers go right ahead and direct the person (**bald-on-record**) by saying something like *Stay home.* Alternatively, a more polite formulation could be used: *Do you mind staying home to help those most vulnerable?* or *Could you please stay home?* Phrases like *do you mind*, *could you* and *please* are all politeness markers of various sorts whose function is to mitigate the threat posed to the addressee, recognising the imposition expressed.

Languages like Japanese, Thai, Chinese, French and German have grammatical markers that are specifically geared up to express politeness, such as special pronouns, **honorifics** (like titles and special words expressing respect) or special verb forms. English does not appear to have such grammatical tools and this has given rise to the myth that English lacks politeness. Do not be fooled, nothing could be further from the truth!

The way in which English speakers show deference or concern for their listeners' face is by using modal verbs like *could* or *might*, politeness phrases like *please, if you don't mind, if it's not too much trouble* and general wordiness. Hints, which are considered **indirect speech acts**, like *Gosh there are so many vulnerable people catching Covid-19* or *We all need to help those less lucky, whose immune systems are compromised* are typical ways for English speakers to show politeness. Indirectness is key in showing respect and recognition of the listener's needs and maintaining harmony.

Let's return to the use of *stay safe* in the context of politeness strategies. As we saw earlier, during the Covid-19 pandemic, many people around the world took to social media to voice various orders, commands and threats containing this phrase. At the same time, the phrase also began to appear on public signage placed in shop windows and on doors of various organisations.

Looking closely at such signage, Eva Ogiermann (2025) observed that the use of the phrase in these signs began to change over time. Initially, *stay safe* was merely a straightforward way of showing concern for the health and safety of others. Organisations were trying to show solidarity with everyday citizens.

However, gradually, as the pandemic spread and as people were being urged to wear masks and practice social distancing, the phrase became a directive, a threat calling for shared responsibility in keeping others safe by adhering to the rules. At the same time, for some members of society, this phrase became increasingly synonymous with government oppression, control and coercion. Suddenly, what was once a kind well-wishing phrase became over time a coercive, oppressive and highly imposing threat. This analysis also illustrates how the illocutionary and perlocutionary acts can shift from one another and from speaker to addressee.

A similar study of Covid-19 language (Han, 2021) analysed directives posted by government organisations on the Chinese platform Weibo. Like Ogiermann, Yanmei Han's data showed that initially, such posts were received positively by the wider public despite their impolite tone. Under normal circumstances, graphic depictions such as those given in (16) would be considered a threat to anyone's face.

(16)

a) 今年上门，明年上坟
Jingnian shangmen, mingnian shangfen
'A visit to others this year means a visit to your grave next year.'

b) 今天到处乱跑，明天坟上长草
Jintian daochu luanpao, mingtian fenshang zhangcao
'Running around today incurs grass growing on your grave tomorrow.'

c) 今天走亲或访友，明天家中剩条狗
Jintian zouqin huo fangyou, mingtian jiazhong sheng tiao gou
'Visiting friends or relatives today results in (the death of the whole family and) only one dog left at home tomorrow.'

Initially, the severity of the situation and gravity of the consequences of Covid-19 were deemed by the public to warrant the strong language used. It was understood as perhaps necessary to achieve a better outcome for all. However, as time passed, people began to react negatively to such strong directives, finding them increasingly impolite and unpalatable.

These examples show that politeness is situational. It is culturally and temporally anchored so that what may be appropriate and inoffensive in one society and at one time can change over the course of history. Language is always on the move, adapting to fit our needs. The ways we use to communicate with one another reflect those changes and as our needs change, so does our language, mirroring societal norms and world views of the time.

WANT MORE?

- Read Yan Huang's book on *Pragmatics* (2013), especially chapters 4–6.
- Watch Lera Boroditsky's 2017 TEDEd talk on how language shapes thought (https://www.ted.com/dubbing/lera_boroditsky_how_language_shapes_the_way_we_think?audio=en&language=en).
- Listen to the *Lingthusiasm* podcast on Gricean Maxims, cooperation and humour (https://www.youtube.com/watch?v=dw46d7I9AEs&list=PLcqOJ708UoXT1KmfcY841iR3vtkXVfi1i&index=1).

5

LANGUAGE YOUR WAY

In May 2025, journalist Andrea Vance (2025) printed an opinion piece in a major New Zealand newspaper featuring the word *cunt* and thereby 'dropping the c-bomb', as the incident became known in the media. One of the ministers mentioned in the piece went on to complain in the upcoming Parliament sitting about this incident and made history by repeating this word as she spoke against 'the clearly gendered and patronising language [. . .] used to reduce senior Cabinet ministers to girlbosses, hype squads, references to girl math and cunts'. This statement sparked nothing short of a media storm. But what is gendered language? Why did this use draw so much attention? And what does the incident say about the kind of English that is used in Aotearoa New Zealand? There is a lot to unpack in this example, so let's begin by looking at gendered language.

GENDERED LANGUAGE

The term **gendered language** refers to usage that encourages and reinforces gender stereotypes (i.e., manly men and girly women). It can also refer to normative behaviour around gender, for example, the assumed existence of only two genders and the erasure or marginalisation of alternate gender categories, like non-binary persons.

One early study in this area dates to the 1970s, when the field of language and gender was just getting started. In her article, American linguist Robin Lakoff argued that the word *widow* (used to refer to women whose husband had passed away) was much more common than the word *widower* (used to refer to men whose wife had

DOI: 10.4324/9781003621485-5

died). It might seem a small matter, but as Lakoff explained, this disparity reinforces societal norms that define women by their material status, in other words, as having been someone's wife even after that man's death. Importantly, the same is not true of men. Their identity does not seem to rely on being an appendage to their (deceased) spouse. Anecdotally, in my experience, media articles also seem to describe women by referring to the number of children they have (*X, mother of three*) while men are described in terms of their profession (*Y, manager of company Z*). Such uses present female and male identities differently, thereby perpetuating outdated stereotypes; that women should be married and have children, that men should be successful businesspeople. Studies investigating perceptions suggest that these subtle cues are not benign but instead, they are stored and internalised, especially with repeated exposure.

Other examples of pairs of words that invite different associations for men and women include *spinster-bachelor* and *master/mistress*. While the female words (*spinster* and *mistress*) have negative connotations, signalling a departure from societal expectations (of marriage), undesirability and promiscuity, their male counterparts (*bachelor* and *master*) conjure positive aspirational notions of freedom, attractiveness and desirability. Considering how language is used to talk about certain groups in society exposes social inequities and sources of bias. **Bias** identification is the first step towards a fairer world, and the study of language can therefore illuminate perceptions, conscious and unconscious, about various social groups.

The language used in films and on the big screen also provides avenues for probing societal norms about different genders. For example, analyses of movie characters have found that female protagonists 'talk' a lot less than male ones. In a recent book on the topic, researchers Carmen Fought and Karen Eisenhauer (2022) investigate the language of Disney movies. Alarmingly, it turns out that not only do female characters have smaller proportions of dialogue compared to their male counterparts, but more than that, the trend only gets worse over time. Speaking time for females portrayed in new versions of various Disney movies since the 1989 remake of the *Little Mermaid* dropped to about 20% or 30% of the total dialogue. Even new movies like *Frozen* (2013) saw males take up 59% of the dialogue. It is quite astonishing to think that the central characters in these movies were meant to be females. What are young girls (and boys) watching these movies learning about being a girl? Apparently, that girls should be seen and not heard, among other things. The patterns are subtle, and we are probably not even consciously aware of them but that does not render their effects less real.

Not all gendered language goes under the radar. Analysing perceptions of trans-gender and non-binary genders online, Lex Konnelly (2022) finds considerable negativity and bias that is very much explicit. An example from the Reddit posts analysed by Konnelly (2022, p. 6) is given in (1); only the first few lines are provided here, but the passage continues in much the same vein.

(1) I know I just went by peta and mark last month but can you guys call me tommy now 🤍🥺🥺 I'll change it again in a month to Kai but please call me tommy now it makes my euphoria go brrrr' 🥺🥺🌸🤍 if you won't call my pronouns cat/catself and refer to me as cat gender you are transphobic, even if you are a dysphoric trans person yourself who transitioned into a male, female, or they/them!!

The post constitutes an offensive enacted characterisation of non-binary and trans people. Its mocking tone ridicules them by suggesting they change their names and pronouns repeatedly and pokes fun at their purported exaggerated femininity, through the use of emotionally coloured emojis and online expressions associated with cuteness (*go brrrr'*). There is also a deliberate misquote of the term *(gender) dysphoria* (a medical condition referring to a person who suffers discomfort or unease in relation to their experienced gender), given in the post as *euphoria* (a state of intense pleasure and happiness). This confused form further plays on their implied confusion.

The passage goes on in this derisive manner, mimicking negative stereotypes present in other spaces, in popular media and offline. Whether direct or indirect, performed gender stereotypes can perpetuate societal norms that marginalise and erase the identities of non-dominant groups.

In reaction to these practices, activists have sought to **reclaim** some of the slurs that have been hurled at them. An example of this is the word *bitch*. Initially, it was used to refer to a female dog, but over time, it became a slur for a promiscuous, angry, stubborn or even violent woman. Over the history of the word, activists have sought to 'rehabilitate' it by encouraging women to use it to refer to themselves or others in a positive way, contesting dominant patriarchal expectations portraying women as submissive and passive. You might also know Meredith Brook's 1997 song *Bitch*, in which she lashes out against societal expectations of the idealised woman, being a *mother*, a *lover*, a *sinner*, a *saint* and so on. Brooks emphasises the multifaceted identities that women are expected to adopt and their contradicting and exhausting nature. These expectations are not just impossibly high to attain but also in contradiction with one another. Efforts to reclaim this particular slur date as far back as the 1960s feminists. Karen Stollznow has published an entire book on the 'word with teeth', as she calls it, and its history (Stollznow, 2024).

That said, the road to reclamation is not equally smooth for all slurs. The word *cunt* presents some difficulties in this respect, possibly because it is perceived as being exceedingly taboo compared to other similar words, but also because it references – not a behaviour (unlike *bitch*) but – a female sexual organ, which is used to reduce females to sexual objects. This means that when a female uses the word, she inevitably denigrates her own person by referencing her anatomy. I return to this word later in this chapter.

PERFORMING GENDER: BAD BITCHES AND CUTE WINSOMENESS

Staying with gender, a second example that Lakoff brought to the fore involved differences in how women and men used language. In particular, she stressed women's avoidance of expletives, strong language, forceful requests and impolite usage. Lakoff explained that women, unlike men, are socialised to steer away from such elements in a bid to present themselves in line with societal norms of what it is to be feminine. Shrill voices and brash language were not seen as becoming of a lady.

Indeed, other scholars have corroborated the general findings that women (in Western cultures) tend to use standard forms of language more often than men. As we saw earlier with various stereotypes of different genders, differences in socialisation between girls and boys can also lead to discrimination and bias. Patterns of linguistic femininity are frequently interpreted as lacking confidence, expertise and authority; precisely the kinds of characteristics that hold women back in positions of leadership.

Only a few years after Lakoff published her landmark article on language and 'woman's place' (now here's a phrase that might raise a few eyebrows), a rising female politician was being made aware of ways in which her language was holding her back. It was around the late 1970s that former British Prime Minister Margaret Thatcher began a series of voice training sessions to increase her political standing. According to her biographer, Charles Moore, the transformation was a huge success. "Soon the hectoring tones of the housewife gave way to softer notes and a smoothness that seldom cracked except under extreme provocation on the floor of the House of Commons", he wrote (according to Gardner, 2014). Apparently, leadership skills stand in direct opposition to 'hectoring tones of the housewife'.

Fast forward a couple of decades and enter a revolutionary new paradigm in how gender itself was to be understood. Associated with scholars like Judith Butler, this new wave of studies saw gender as something one does, rather than something one is. This became known as the **performativity theory of gender**. Crucially, in this new theory, gender is seen not as a deterministic binary opposition, specified by our genetic code, but as a social enterprise, open to negotiation in interaction.

For example, mothers talking with their infants might use linguistic elements associated with feminine repertoires, baby talk like *bunny* and *teddy*, uptalk (termed **high rising intonation**) and tag questions (*isn't it?* and *should we?*). Similarly, when messaging close (girl)friends, women might employ communication elements emphasising solidarity and vulnerability: *oh that is like soooo cuuuute* ❀♡ *!!!*, by using emojis, elongated vowel spellings, filler words (*like*) and exclamation marks. Such language helps to perform the role of mother or that of a close friend.

Importantly, these repertoires are equally available to men. And research tells us that indeed men also use emojis, *like* and other filler words as well as baby talk – it just depends on the situation, who they are talking with and how they wish to present themselves. These uses are not about biology but about context and relationships.

If we change the setting to a boardroom meeting, the (same) women might perform what would otherwise be associated with a masculine repertoire, namely use commanding and authoritative, unapologetic language. Sentences like *I think it might be good to perhaps invest in these stocks* might become *I want us to shift to these stocks now*.

In short, gender is not fixed but malleable, and different speakers perform different styles, depending on the role they want to emphasise in each situation. While we can still talk about feminine ways of speaking vis-à-vis masculine ways of speaking, these are not exclusively used by women or men, but available to all genders.

Moreover, there is no single way of 'doing' femininity or masculinity; but rather multiple ways of performing these. Let's consider performed femininity as observed in the South Korean phenomenon of *aegyo*. *Aegyo* translates into English as winsomeness and performed cuteness. The meaning of the word itself comes from its structural parts: *ae* (愛) 'love' and *gyo* (嬌) 'charming, bewitching'.

Aegyo manifests itself in various ways, from the adoption of certain cutified and infantilised fashions, accompanied by matching gestures and acts like mimicking pet behaviour, clapping repeatedly and excitedly in a child-like fashion, deliberate clumsiness, pouting of lips, stomping of feet, tantrums, but also linguistic features like high-pitched voice, whispering, using baby talk or diminutive cutesy words.

Aljosa Puzar and Yewon Hong (2018) describe *aegyo* as a tactical tool which (particularly young) Korean women adopt to get ahead in life, both at home, in the context of romantic partnerships but also at work, among work colleagues in formal settings. Ideologically, *aegyo* constitutes an attempt to redress power imbalances within a strongly patriarchal, androcentric and ageist society. This is done not by contesting these notions and attempting to overturn them but by playing into their hand and increasing the speaker's capacity for being liked and desired.

In their study of the phenomenon, Puzar and Hong conducted semi-structured interviews and questionnaires with both female and male South Koreans. They discovered that the dollification of the South Korean woman into a passive, excessively winsome and lovable creature was viewed positively by both genders. Interestingly, women saw *aegyo* as a strategic resource to be mastered, a skill to be used to the advantage of the female enacting it. In contrast, men downplayed performative aspects of the role, seeing it as a natural aspirational quality (that perhaps some were even born with), associated with likeability and desirability.

The cuteness and winsomeness of South Korean women parallels other similar notions found throughout East Asia. These include the Chinese concept of *sajiao* (撒娇) and the Japanese notion of *amae* (甘え). Both ideas reference notions of infantilisation and dependency on others, be they fathers, husbands or superiors. Puzar and Hong explain that women with *amae* or *sajiiao* need protection, love and care and the enaction of these values further propagates patriarchal relations of power.

In stark contrast to the winsome *aegyo* persona, we find a completely different Korean female identity rooted in K-pop tropes: the *gijibae* 'bad girl'. Almost diametrically opposed, the *gijibae* is "an aggressive, sexually agentive and polemical figure of racialised womanhood from US hip hop", explains Joyhanna Yoo Garza (2021, p. 24). *Gijibae* emulates the *Bad Bitch* persona, a symbol of empowered, streetwise femininity that appropriates elements of African Vernacular American English (AAVE), combining racialised cultural elements borrowed from Black and Brown hip-hop artists with features associated with Western culture.

Doing the *Bad Bitch* involves adopting various aspects of self-presentation; from fashion (wearing gold chains and American-style baseball caps) to visual effects (spinning baseballs and engaging in activities associated with freedom and pleasure) and language use (for instance, the language used in song lyrics). K-pop songs often contain a mix of Korean and English, as you might hear, for example, in the lyrics of the K-pop star CL (Garza, 2021, p. 10).

Garza zooms in on CL's music to show how this might be done. In one particular song, the Korean title (*Nappeun gijibae*) is accompanied by an English one alongside it (*The baddest female*). Moreover, the lyrics combine Korean and English words and the English used is itself a mix of standard grammar (*stand up right now*) interspersed with elements of non-standard grammar found in AAVE (the title itself *baddest*, and lines like *where all my bad girls at*). The presence of AAVE acts as a symbolic resource which emulates the style of American hip-hop artists and presents the singer as sharing similar characteristics: modernity, street-knowledge, fierceness and rebellion. The adoption of English represents an aspiration to affiliate with a global discourse, an arena dominated by English (see Chapters 6 and 9 for more on language mixing). Finally, the meaning of the lyrics is confronting, direct and authoritative, having virtually nothing in common with the values of the *aegyo* persona.

These diametrically opposed sets of enactments speak to the idea that gender is not a set of permanent characteristics, which are somehow betrayed by language (or other resources). At the same time, the linguistic features, fashions and other self-presentation aspects of various groups become associated with the varying repertoires adopted by those enacting them (termed **indexing**), which then allows individuals to use them to position themselves as members within such groups. This self-enforcing mechanism is constantly evolving across societies and time.

We saw earlier the use of AAVE by people who are not of African American descent. Here is another group of speakers who are neither American, nor Black (or Brown) and who use features of AAVE in their language: White British gay men. Christian Ilbury has collected a large body of tweets (back when Twitter was not yet X) posted by White British gay men and discovered precisely this kind of use, see (2) for some of his examples (2019, pp. 9–10).

(2)

(a) Sat **Sippin'** ma Starbucks in Soho Square with @User #london #soho #sohosquare #relax
(b) Post swim, gym and steam.... Feeling pumped for another night in the big city working **dat** podium!
(c) @User@User y'all need to have a drink. **Lawd** knows y'all thirsty!
(d) When I wake up and there no text from **bae**! And then suddenly remembering the fact there i have no **bae**....
(e) My bitches working **them** boots #Gucci #glamsquad #dubai #mydubai #friends #fashionista

For ease of identification, Ilbury bolds elements that are lifted from AAVE, for example words spelled in the way they might be pronounced in AAVE, like *Sippin'* ('sipping'), *dat* ('that') and *Lawd* ('Lord'), terms of affection like *bae* and non-standard grammar forms like *working them boots*.

Why would a White British gay man use AAVE? Like the Korean *gijibae* uses, the language here also draws on associations with the AAVE persona, albeit a slightly different but overlapping set of associations: the independent, flamboyant, sassy Black woman. The marginalised status of Black women, together with their fierce resilience and unapologetic capacity for survival in the face of pervasive and dominant oppression, makes their repertoire a fitting emblem for a group of people – gay men – who see themselves as embodying similar characteristics of oppression and resilience. This linguistic vehicle gives rise to the Sassy Queen persona, by now, a well-established repertoire used by gay men online and offline.

Feminine ways of speaking have long been associated with male sexuality, according to Evan Hazenberg (2020). For example, in English, these might be highly specific colour terms like *magenta* or *periwinkle*, adjectives like *fabulous* and *divine,* frequent use of exclamation marks and effeminate terms of address like *darling* and *girlfriend*. There are also phonological features, such as the change of *said* to *thaid* and *sound* into *thound*, pejoratively known as the 'the gay lisp'. According to Hazenberg the difference between these sounds (S and TH) is down to tongue position and it is something we can objectively measure by recording speakers and then inspecting their sound frequencies. Some studies have shown that indeed, there are differences of this type in several varieties of English in America, Canada and New Zealand, however, the differences are negligible in other languages, such as Japanese and German. This means that they are not consistent throughout the world's languages. They are, like other aspects discussed so far, part of a performed repertoire used to index an identity rather than a biologically determined trait.

It is revealing to take stock of just how far-removed *aegyo, gijibae* and *Sassy Queens* are from traditional and outdated notions of 'hectoring tones of the housewife'. It is becoming increasingly clear that performative theories of gender have been instrumental in explaining, not just the construction of feminine and masculine identities, but also the construction of non-binary identities, as well as lesbian and gay repertoires. Can you tell someone's sexuality or gender from the way they speak? That depends on whether they want you to and whether you are sufficiently familiar with the repertoire of the respective sexuality or gender to recognise the cues associated with it.

These insights tell us that not all members of the group are the same; not all gay males use the same repertoire and signal their sexuality in the same way; they may choose to conceal it in certain situations and foreground it in others. The same goes for women and non-binary people. Crucially, linguistic cues are just that: cues, and not immutable traits.

'DOING' RACE AND NATION: SPEAKING BLACK, SPEAKING SERBIAN

The previous examples brought into focus a recurring aspect of identity performance: being Black/Brown. We saw how Korean K-pop singers enlist features from AAVE to index the Bad Bitch persona and how White British gay men use AAVE features to bring to life the Sassy Queen. Both groups embody various characteristics (resilience, marginalisation, aggression, independence) associated with this unrelated racial group to perform a specific identity.

Let's consider AAVE more closely. We have already seen that individuals who are not of African American descent sometimes use the variety. Conversely, not all African American people use it, and even those that do, don't use it in all contexts. Research has consistently shown that using features associated with AAVE, like double negation (*I haven't seen none of those people before*), deletion of third person *-s* (*He come down the town every Sunday*) and copula deletion (*He seen me before*) is likely to lead to **linguistic discrimination**.

Indeed, it was anger and shock at the persistent and widespread discrimination directed at AAVE speakers that kickstarted linguistics work in this area in the first place. In the 1960s, Bill Labov and others like him set out to overturn myths surrounding racialised ways of speaking English. One early aim was to redress inequalities suffered by African American children, whose language was deemed inferior within the dominant White structures of power circulating in the American school system at the time. Deficient speech was deemed to betray deficient minds and thus lead to poor outcomes. In reality, linguistic discrimination aimed at a specific group of children was instrumental in holding them back.

The course of the following 60 years showed that from housing to employment, schooling and the law, AAVE speakers were being marginalised and misrepresented in all sorts of ways, most of which had nothing to do with language. 'Sounding Black' led to rental flats being taken, jobs being filled and court witness statements being misunderstood or discounted.

But much like gender and sexuality construction, ethnicity is also linked to identity performance. Speakers can master and use multiple **ethnolinguistic varieties** and switch between them as the context demands. For instance, former president Barack Obama was heard switching from standard American English speech to AAVE while addressing a Black American cashier in Washington, DC in 2009 (uttering *Nah, we straight* in response to being offered change for his purchase). My 3rd-year sociolinguistics students are consistently surprised to learn that the sound recordings I play during class of former United States Secretary of State Condoleezza Rice constitute the speech of an African American speaker, not that of a White American speaker. Like Margaret Thatcher, these politicians may have learnt to adapt their speech if they were to appeal to a wider group of voters.

While ethnic ways of speaking can be appropriated to create personae associated with traits or characteristics of their speakers, like being fierce and independent, the converse has also been observed. For example, certain sexualities have been appropriated in a bid to transfer desirable ideologies linked to them to a particular ethnic group or even an entire nation.

Here is an example in which queer sexualities are used to **index** (act as a proxy for) progressive and tolerant nation-states. Scanning tourist advertisements from Cape Town, Joseph Comer (2018) brings examples of visual and linguistic elements associated with gay culture that are used as symbols of a liberal and exotic tourist destination. The identity of Cape Town as *Africa's gay capital* is enacted through a series of pinkwashing rhetorical resources: using the colour pink throughout the ads to show affinity with gay communities, referencing gay personalities like Elton John and stereotyped camp sexual innuendos, words like *pride*, *Rainbow* and phrases like *glam-to-the-max*, *Sex on the Beach*, *gagging for more*. Two examples are given in (3) and (4) from Comer (2018, pp. 67 and 74), obtained from the travel sites RhinoAfrica.com and Out2Africa.com, respectively:

(3) Cape Town is one of the gay capitals of the world! No wonder Elton John has a couple of favourite places to visit on our

website (if you ask us nicely we'll tell you where!) – it is hard to imagine a more liberal, diverse and accepting society.

(4) Whether it's a Manhattan you want or good old Sex on the Beach, Cape Town is a cocktail of sights and sounds that will leave you gagging for more. Luxury apartments and boutique hotels, glamorous sidewalk cafés and a feast of restaurants, bars and late night venues are all part of the cities [sic] vibrant gay culture. [...]

The ads are accompanied by predominantly White and masculine bodies, bearing little connection to the true ethnic makeup of the city. This constructed image of Cape Town commodifies queer identities in an effort to replace negative perceptions of the entire country – Cape Town is seen as a bastion for South Africa as a whole – with associations of a tolerant, progressive and Westernised nation. We have the best gays here, that is how modern and progressive we are!

The relationship between nationality and ethnicity is often complex and variable. But just imagine how much more complex these identities might be for a teenager growing up in a war-torn country. One study of teenagers coming of age in Belgrade exposed the strategic way that they used language to navigate their conflicting and emerging identities online. As speakers of Serbian and avid users of social media, these teenagers faced various existential questions regarding their affiliation locally, nationally and globally. The internal conflicts are also evident in their language choices.

Before looking at their language, let me set the scene and the context of their interactions. Despite having different names, Serbian and Croatian are for all intents and purposes mutually intelligible languages. Yet they remain symbolic icons of the ethnic and national groups of speakers who use them. Additionally, Serbian presents a duality in its spelling because it can be written in both the Cyrillic and the Latin alphabet. Writers can choose which script to use.

Historically, Cyrillic was emblematically associated with Serbian nationalism, and for the Croat population, with Serbian dominance and oppression. Since the Balkan Wars, these beliefs have been accentuated following the split of the country. Serbian continued to use both alphabets, but Cyrillic was hailed as the higher-status choice. As a bastion of national pride, Cyrillic was also seen as a symbol of detachment from the West, for example, from countries like America and its allies, who bombed Serbia in the late 1990s. On a personal level, the Balkan Wars have left many Serbians feeling ostracised and resentful, with relations remaining frosty between Serbia and Western powers. Young people growing up in the post-1990 era were stuck in the middle of a conflict they did not create, but one in which they struggled to find a place.

Navigating identity matters during adolescence is difficult enough as it is without adding a larger looming controversy about one's country and ethnic group. Rachel George (2020) studied some of the language used by Serbian teenagers online, discussing the various options at their disposal. One is to use the Cyrillic script, another is to use the Latin script, except that the latter comes with further options; either to use a script containing Serbian accents (**diacritics**) like đ (pronounced like J or DJ in English *judge*), č (pronounced like CH in English *church*) or š (pronounced like SH in English *sharp*), or to use a simplified Latin script containing the kinds of letters that English uses (no diacritics). In addition to Serbian, the teenagers surveyed by George also used English words, which came with their own spelling choices.

Leaving the English words aside, let's concentrate on the Serbian text. Which script did Belgrade teenagers favour in their Facebook posts and why? The answer is all of them. Significantly, the presence of the various scripts was symbolic and performative, not random. Cyrillic was less prevalent, being **marked** (not the default option) and used, for example, to make bold anti-Western statements, to reference national topics like national holidays, but also sometimes to satirise and mock over the top, formal Serbian customs.

In one meme (Figure 5.1), students used an image of the American rapper Snoop Dogg, accompanied by the message *Hristizl se rodizl; vaistinizl se rodizl* ('Christ is born/Indeed he is born') given in Cyrillic script.

This message represents a common Orthodox Easter greeting, rooted in religious tradition. What is more, the Cyrillic spelling was further altered in the meme by adding (in Cyrillic letters) the **suffix** *-iz* or *-izl* at the end of the words, a phenomenon associated with 'Snoop talk'.

This symbolic, performative language helped to juxtapose tradition (religious greetings), nationalism (Cyrillic script) and modernity

Figure 5.1 Serbian meme used on Facebook

Source: George (2020, p. 411). Reproduced with permission, origin unknown

(unconventional, modified spelling) with global affiliation (referencing a Western cultural icon and his new associated way of speaking). Teenagers used this complex but effective strategy of remixing language resources as a way of asserting simultaneous identities, on the one hand, their Serbian identity (it would be impossible to understand the meme without knowledge of the Cyrillic script) and, on the other, their global identity (by showing familiarity with global icons and modern takes on their speech).

In another example (George, 2022, p. 414), when a teenager uses the Latin alphabet containing single letters where the diacritics have been left out (***S**to* 'what'), the reply comes back with a clever double-meaning. It contains double letters (*zna**sh*** 'know' and ***sh**ta* 'what') rather than single ones, thereby signalling a further break away from traditional Serbian spelling rules. What is going on?

(5) A. ***Sto*** *si me zaboravila, bona?*
'What, did you forget me dear?'
B. *Ti **znash** da ja tebe nikada ne mogu da zaboravim…**shta** ima*
'You know that I would never forget you…what's up?'

The choice to spell words with a single letter follows the Serbian tenet of one-sound-one-letter, albeit without the diacritics. In contrast, using double letters breaks further away from Serbian rules, in that it breaks away from the one-to-one correspondence between letter and sound, as well as leaving out the diacritics. This move is interpreted as being closer to English spelling and thus as an affront to (the sometimes serious and heavily rule-governed) Serbian ideology. The reply conveys the intended message 'yes I care' as well as a gentle 'just lighten up' overtone.

George explains that Serbian language ideology sees the one-to-one relationship between sound and spelling as confirmation of the superiority of the language. It is funny to consider how defensive British English prescriptivists are about the non-intuitive spelling of English words (just imagine the horror of leaving out all those silent letters!), seeing them as a bastion of 'proper English'. Meanwhile, in other parts of the world, what counts as a marker of pride is precisely the opposite way around.

Although we like to pigeonhole others in immutable categories, it is clear that just about any identity can be performed, from gender to sexuality, race and ethnicity. Performing various identities is not limited to individuals but can be extended to larger social groups, including entire nations. Language variation is observed not just between individuals but also across regions and countries.

LANGUAGE IN YOUR AREA: REGIONAL VARIATION

Returning to Andrea Vance's transgression and her use of the c-word, one question which journalists wanted to know at the time was why did this happen in Aotearoa New Zealand? Could this have happened anywhere else and are New Zealanders just more potty-mouthed than other English speakers?

Along with national pride, we sometimes also find a strong dollop of **linguistic insecurity** (negative feelings about one's language variety). Countries like Aotearoa New Zealand and Singapore have long histories of feelings of insecurity surrounding the way their citizens speak English. To be clear, this is not about **linguistic proficiency**, feeling insecure about being a non-native speaker of a language, but general feelings that one's native variety is somehow deficient.

For many years, prescriptivists purported that British English, or even the Queen's English or Received Pronunciation, was 'the proper way' to speak the language. Britain was, after all, where the language first originated. For more preposterous language attitudes and rebuttals to this idea, see Chapter 9. For now, let's focus on the differences between different varieties of the same language.

Deborah Cameron writes in her 2023 book that in the United States, only a few years prior to the Aotearoa New Zealand Parliament incident, an American comedian referred to one of Trump's daughters as *a fecking cunt*, which led to a strong chorus of disapproval, forcing her to issue a public apology. To my knowledge, no such apology was ever issued by Andrea Vance. American English speakers appear to be more conservative when it comes to the c-word. Fortunately for New Zealand English speakers, Martin Schweinberger and Kate Burridge (2025a) published a well-timed article only a few months after the Parliament incident, confirming that Americans, Brits and Australians used – overall – more profane words than New Zealanders, at least online, so the country breathed a collective sigh of relief.

Profanity aside, **regional variation**, that is, variation in how a (single) language is spoken in different places around the world, runs much deeper than varying patterns of taboo words. One important issue to sort out is the difference between a language and a dialect – a notoriously difficult task. If in the past, 'a language was a dialect with an army and a navy' (often attributed to Max Weinreich but possibly misquoted), today, a language is probably a dialect with Google searchability. The point is that drawing the line between languages and dialects is often arbitrary. The distinction is typically not made on linguistic grounds but on political, social or economic grounds.

If you ever learnt Italian as a foreign language, you would have been taught standard Italian, even though your teacher is unlikely to have ever used that term. Italian is not one language, it is many. There are at least six major varieties of Italian: Corsican, Friulian, Ladin, Sardinian, Tuscan and Venetian, and they each have their own sub-dialects. Standard Italian is based on Tuscan though I have not seen any Italian language classes advertising Tuscan Italian. Are all these Italian languages mutually intelligible? Well, that depends on who is talking to whom and on how hard they are trying to understand each other.

When I was taking French classes in high school, no one asked me which kind of French I was learning. I just learnt what everyone called 'French'. Except that isn't one language either, it is also many: there is standard French (Parisian would probably be the best label for it, referencing the region where it is typically spoken), Belgium French, Swiss French, Canadian French, Mauritian French, Algerian French, Moroccan French, Haitian French, Indian French, Vietnamese French, New Caledonian French and we have not even got to French dialects spoken within France itself. Mutual intelligibility is also a matter of degree here: Canadian French movies are notoriously known for being subtitled in France.

It takes no history buff to see what is going on here. Wherever French armies and colonisers went, so did their language. For some speakers, these varieties of French represent a conflicting mix of pride in speaking a local version of French, but they also bear the scars of colonisation, in being able to only speak the coloniser's language and not one's own **heritage language**.

While some regional dialects are fighting to be recognised as languages in their own right, others remain politically stranded: think Korean in South and North Korea. Although the two languages are mutually intelligible, extreme nationalism and totalitarian state politics dictate that they are distinct languages. In 2023, North Korea sentenced 20 young athletes (skiers) to hard labour prison camps for a period of 3–5 years 'for speaking like South Koreans', according to an article by Jieun Kim for *Radio Free Asia (Korean)*. This move is part of the North Korean government's attempt to control and stamp out all capitalist influence from the country, from food and soap operas all the way to vowels and consonants. Clearly, such linguistic separation between North and South Korean languages is ideologically driven and not linguistically motivated.

At the end of the day, language is spoken by people in the way that they choose to speak it. Enforcing new-speak doctrines never works, or at least never works for long. As speakers of certain languages, be they English, Italian, French or Korean, we have the feeling that we all speak the same language, however, we each put our own spin on the way that we speak it in order to signal our varying identities and if you look closely enough, no two speakers sound exactly the same as each other.

WANT MORE?

- Read Deborah Cameron's book *Language, Sexism and Misogyny* (2023).
- Check out the *Conversation* story on *201 ways to say 'fuck'* by Martin Schweinberger and Kate Burridge (2025b).
- Listen to Christian Ilbury talk about language variation online in the (2025) Lexis Podcast (https://podcasts.apple.com/gb/podcast/episode-55-christian-ilbury-and-online-language/id1517687490?i=1000654052855)

6

LANGUAGE ON THE MOVE

Many people are aware that language changes and they are often not too pleased about it. Will change dilute and erode language as we know it to a point of no return? Highly unlikely. Not only is change a natural process but in many cases, it is also vital or at least, much needed.

The most obvious type of change involves words: new words come into use, existing words go out of use, and meanings of existing words change so that the words begin to feel new again. Such changes are humorously illustrated in Joseph Ducreux Rap memes (Figure 6.1), which 'translate' modern-day rap songs into their perceived Old English equivalent (not always correctly!), imposed on the image of Joseph Ducreux, the eighteenth-century French painter known for his Avangard style. Can you guess the song referenced? It is indeed *Who let the dogs out*.

However, this is not the only aspect of a language that changes: from how we pronounce words and spell them, all the way to how we structure phrases and texts, languages never stand still.

Yet there is also a tension between change and resistance to it because too much change would result in an unusable system of communication; and this is what some fear. On the other hand, stagnation does not allow for communication to grow and adapt to our changing modern world. But where does change come from and how does it unfold?

DOI: 10.4324/9781003621485-6

Figure 6.1 Joseph Ducreux rap meme

Source: Know Your Meme – https://knowyourmeme.com/memes/joseph-ducreux-archaic-rap

LANGUAGE IN THE CITY: URBAN CENTRES AS HUBS OF CHANGE

Let's begin by considering a place of bustling language change: the big city. Urban centres are known to encourage and expedite language change in light of their diverse and large populations, especially in places that see ongoing migration. Cities like Berlin, London, Copenhagen and Stockholm are hotbeds for new dialects, which diverge from the majority language (Kerswill & Weise, 2022). These dialects are associated with the language of the youth, who are known to be drivers of change.

Consider Berlin. This big city is the home of a new variety called *Kiezdeutsch*, literally 'neighbourhood German', which has emerged as a new repertoire of choice for tight-knit social groups living and interacting in the inner city. German linguist Heike Wiese (2009, 2015) has researched this dialect for over a decade, investigating its origins, features and status.

Being a large central-European country with a population of over 83 million inhabitants, Germany is what some term a **monolingual habitus** place. That means the country operates from the assumption of a largely monolingual mode, in which the default code of communication is standard German or *Hochdeutsch*, as the locals call it. If you walk into a shop, bank or school, the expectation is that you will use and be addressed in Hochdeutsch. The meaning of the label is itself telling. Comprising two words, Hochdeutsch means 'high' (*hoch*) + 'German' (*Deutsch*). Although that may not have been its origin, these days, the word stands for 'the better' and 'superior' version of German, the one that everyone should aim to speak. Labels are not neutral; they impact how speakers come to think of what they are describing. The dominant status of standard German comes at the marginalisation of other varieties (see Chapter 9 for more on attitudes).

By contrast, Kiezdeutsch is the street code that circulates among urban youth wanting to connect and share lived experiences in large cities, whose linguistic makeup is nothing like the monolingual default implied by Hochdeutsch. According to the German census cited by Heike Wiese (2015), 46% of Germans under 18 grow up in multilingual families with a heritage language other than German spoken at home – that's almost half of all young people in the country. This data came from the 2009 to 2010 census, with more recent Migration statistics released by the German Federal Government describing 'historically high immigration' records, suggesting those figures could be even higher today (German Federal Government, 2022). As most migration tends to cluster in large urban centres where job and housing opportunities abound, it becomes evident that a monolingual habitus does not adequately capture the reality of the big German city.

Children growing up in such multilingual environments bring their heritage languages, be they Arabic, Turkish, Polish, Russian, Ukrainian or others, everywhere they go, taking these out of their homes and into schools, playgrounds, local clubs and other public places. In addition, there are also children with monolingual German backgrounds, whose families move to the big city in search of better job opportunities. They bring regional dialect features, different accents and distinct words from those used in Hochdeutsch. Features from these languages and varieties become adopted, blended and remixed within the standard German code to create a new urban **vernacular** dialect. And so, a new dialect is born.

Berlin is not unique in this. Travelling across the Channel to the British Isles, we see a similar situation emerging. The great city of London, a sprawling beast with nearly ten million people is the home of a distinct urban dialect: Multicultural London English. Jenny Cheshire, Paul Kerswill, Susan Fox and Eivind Torgersen have been investigating this repertoire since the early 2000s and according to them, Multicultural London English is replacing other existing London dialects, including Cockney (2013). Similarly to Kiezdeutsch, this way of speaking combines remixed and recycled elements borrowed from migrant languages found in the area alongside features adopted from regional English dialects.

It seems Multicultural London English, or MLE for short, first took off in the London borough of Hackney, driven by adolescents growing up in a mix of backgrounds, from postcolonial varieties of English, Pakistani English, Chinese to Indian, Nigerian and Caribbean English varieties, as well as other migrant languages like Colombian, Albanian, Serbian, Maltese, Portuguese and Spanish.

The heavy Jamaican English influence on MLE had initially earned it the label 'Jafaican'. Similarly to Kiezdeutsch, MLE is associated with being street-smart and having urban in-group kudos, incorporated in lyrics of grime music rising to popularity in East London, cult films depicting inner city London lived experiences as well as advertisements of mobile phones and label trainers.

Although in both of these urban vernaculars, we can identify one language that appears to be central as a source of variation compared to others, Jamaican in the case of MLE and Turkish in the case of Kiezdeutsch, there is no specific target language that drives the direction of change. The emerging new ways of speaking are characterised by two main factors. First, there is variation, lots of different words, sounds and ways of pronouncing new forms abound. Secondly, there is tolerance for variation, many of these innovations are welcome and not under scrutiny by say media, the law or education bodies in the way that we find in standard varieties of a given language. It is this bustling variation and positive attitudes towards it that drive the dynamic and fast-paced level of language change in these urban dialects.

A third dimension which both MLE and Kiezdeutsch share is the association with marginalisation and disadvantage. The background of MLE speakers is typically working class, many speakers are part of violent gangs, some come from broken homes, and typical speakers of Kiezdeutsch live in similarly deprived conditions. Their repertoire is strongly associated with anti-racial discourse and with an inclusive and tolerant worldview of acceptance, positioning itself in opposition to a monolingual, monocultural hegemonic state view.

And as already stated, London and Berlin are by no means unusual when it comes to being hotbeds of language change. But they are great examples of how new ways of speaking change in situations of contact between speakers from different linguistic backgrounds, a field termed **language contact**. While the exact details and contexts of large urban centres around the world vary, we find recurrent similarities in the dynamics of the evolving new repertoires emerging within them.

WHAT CHANGES? EVERYTHING, FROM SOUND TO STRUCTURE

So, how is Kiezdeutsch different from standard German? And what makes MLE distinct from standard British English?

Although Kiezdeutsch is heavily based on standard German, it is German with a twist. Twists at every language level in fact, from sound to word and structure. Heike Wiese and her colleagues (cited in Weise, 2009, and Şimşek & Wiese, 2022) provide examples of words adopted from other languages, such as Turkish *lan* meaning 'man' used in insults or threats *Siktir, lan!* 'Fuck off man!' or Arabic *wallah billa* 'I swear, in God's name', or simply *wallah* (also found in Kurdish and Turkish) to mean something like 'for real'.

Grammatically and morphologically speaking, there are also reductions and rearrangements in word order. For instance, the standard German phrase *keine Kinder* 'no children' is shortened to *kein Kinder* in Kiezdeutsch (reducing the final vowel) and *meine Schwester* 'my sister' becomes *mein Schwester*. On the other hand, it's not just about reductions and deletions: *dein Fitnesscenter* 'your fitness centre' becomes *deine Fitnesscenter*, where an extra *-e* is added.

Determiners (words like *the* and *a*) are left out so that *in den garten* becomes simply *garten* (example as given in Şimşek & Wiese's, 2022, p. 308, ignoring capitalisation spelling rules):

(1) *gehst dy nächstes wochenende eigentlich wieder garten?*
'Are you going to the garden next weekend again?'

The same happens to certain **personal pronouns**, the word *ihn* 'it' would be required in standard German after the verb *wirft* 'throws' but it is omitted in Kiezdeutsch (Şimşek & Wiese, 2022, p. 308):

(2) *er wirft immer runter*
'he throws it always down'

Like in English, standard German contains something called an **existential construction**. These are sentences that start with *there is*, *there are* or simply *there's*. In German, you would use the phrase *es gibt* 'it gives' or *gibt es* when used within a sentence rather than at the beginning of one, but in Kiezdeutsch, the existential is contracted to *gibs*. Similarly, a phrase like *lass uns mal* 'let us' becomes fused as *lassma*.

One final example, standard German has a rule whereby the main verb is placed in second position within **declarative main clauses**, clauses which express the main proposition. This ordering rule is relaxed in Kiezdeutsch. A clause like (3a) would have the **auxiliary** verb *hat* 'has', which helps to make *hat geblockt* 'has blocked' in second position, right after *dannach* 'afterwards'. Instead, it becomes as given in (3b) with the auxiliary in third position, after the subject *sie* 'she' (Şimşek & Wiese, 2022, p. 308):

(3a)	*dannach*	*hat*	*sie*	*mich*	*auch*	*geblockt*
	'afterwards	has	she	me	also	blocked'
(3b)	*dannach*	*sie*	*hat*	*misch*	*auch*	*geblockt*
	'afterwards	she	has	me	also	blocked'

Speakers of standard German will also note the unusual spelling in (3b). The pronoun *mich* 'me' in (3a) is pronounced as *misch* in

Kiezdeutsch (hence the altered spelling). Small but pervasive features of Kiezdeutsch mark it as distinct from Hochdeutsch. It's still German, but German with modifications.

This same situation has also been observed in MLE. There too, building on standard southern British English, a new way of speaking has emerged, with variations in pronunciation, word use and discourse structure.

Here also, we are dealing with a **multiethnolect** variety because the sources contributing variants into the feature pool of this repertoire do not come from a single ethnic group, but from multiple ethnic groups. This contrasts with Chicano English spoken by certain Americans of Mexican origin within areas of the United States, which are **ethnolects** (and have single ethnic group sources).

According to Jenny Cheshire and her colleagues (Cheshire et al., 2022), MLE involves changes in how vowels are pronounced, for example, some **diphthongs** (combinations of vowel sounds where the tongue starts out in one vowel position and ends in another) in words like *face* and *goat* are pronounced higher in the mouth (called **raised** position). There are also changes in how consonants are pronounced, such as the pronunciation of K further back in the mouth in what we call the **uvular** position. The TH sound in words like *thief* and *thing* comes closer to a T sound and in words like *this* and *that* becomes more like D.

Other features include the use of the **indefinite determiner** *a* before all nouns, including those starting with a vowel, so *a banana*, *a house* but also *a apple*, *a egg*. The same pattern affects the **definite determiner** *the*, in which one form is used with all nouns, regardless of whether they begin with a vowel (the same *the* is used with *banana, house, apple* and *egg*).

New MLE lexical items include the innovative use of the word *man* as a first-person pronoun, see the sentence in (4) from Cheshire et al. (2022, p. 5), and borrowings from Jamaican English, words like *bruv* 'brother', *ends* 'neighbourhood' and *whagwan* 'what's up' and other migrant languages like Arabic and Turkish, including *wallah* 'by God, I swear'.

(4) I don't care what my girl looks like…it's her personality man's looking at

Another MLE feature is the novel **quotative** (construction which introduces what someone has said or thought) *this is me* and related variants of it, like *this is him*, *this is her*, more generally captured by the formula [*this is* + speaker]. Here are some examples from the same authors:

(5) this is me "let's go now"
(6) this is him "I've never seen a girl like it"
(7) this is my mum "what are you doing? I was in the queue before you"

As variation is key to new vernaculars, it follows that linguistic innovations arise quickly and can equally quickly fade away into disuse. Moreover, MLE and Kiezdeutsch are by no means exceptions, similar trends have been observed in relation to *Rinkebysvenska* in Stockholm, *Straattaal* in Amsterdam, *Jallanorsk* in Norway or *Københavnsk multietnolekt* in Copenhagen (Cheshire et al., 2013, p. 63).

Moreover, I suspect this trend transcends the big city. As many young people are not just functioning and communicating within their immediate neighbourhoods and boroughs but also frequenting online spaces through the access of social media, we also see an increase in a global vernacular repertoire. In other words, we can see some of these same features pop up and infiltrate geographically dispersed but virtually connected spaces. For example, as my own children reliably inform me, young New Zealand primary-aged children living 10,000 km away from London can also be heard using the word *wallah*, a shared slang term with both MLE and Kiezdeutsch.

WHEN WHOLE NEW LANGUAGES EMERGE

Although both MLE and Kiezdeutsch are distinct from the dominant (standard) languages spoken in their respective countries, they are nevertheless dialects of these languages; MLE is a kind of English, and Kiezdeutsch is a kind of German.

Sometimes, situations of language contact can lead to bigger things than new dialects: they can also lead to entirely new languages, which are sufficiently distinct from the languages that give rise to them that they are not dialects ('a type') of either language.

For example, have you ever heard anyone speaking *Kreyòl Ayisyen* (or simply *Kreyòl* for short)? Haitian Creole – as English speakers know it – is spoken by approximately 11 million people, most of whom live in the third largest country in the Caribbean, Haiti (Fattier, 2013).

Following the pre-Colombian era which saw many of the Indigenous Taíno population of Haiti dwindle in numbers following ongoing conflict, forced labour and disease (smallpox in particular), the country came into French hands during the seventeenth century. It was at this time that French colonisers commenced a rich economy of indigo, coffee, sugar, cotton and cocoa plantations. But plantations needed workers and so African slaves were brought in to fill this need. They were speakers of various Bantu languages including Fon, Fon Gbe and Kwa and dialects of these. According to Michel DeGraff (2007, p. 102), a respected Haitian Creole scholar, in 1681, the slave population numbered only about 2,000 people, amounting to 30% of the country's total, but by 1791, it had grown to 700,00, a staggering 92%.

Communication between French and African speakers paved the way for a whole new language. At its inception, Kreyòl (Haitian Creole) combined linguistic features from the languages that gave rise to it: generally speaking, many words came from French (the lexifier, the **superstrate**), while much of the syntax came from African languages, particularly Kwa dialects (the **substrate**).

According to DeGraff and other scholars, as the country shifted from bilingual speakers (French/Kreyòl and African languages/Kreyòl), towards Kreyòl monolingualism, **neologisms** (new words) moved away from a strong French influence. Importantly, Kreyòl is not a type of insert-any-African-language-here or a type of French, it is completely different from both languages. To convince yourself of this, you can access freely available recordings of Kreyòl speakers at the online *Atlas of Pidgin and Creole Language structures* (APiCS) compiled by Susanne Michaelis and her colleagues.

Here are some examples of Kreyòl from Michel DeGraff's work (2007, pp. 103, 106). Here, I provide the original Kreyòl, a second tier with a more literal translation of the equivalent elements and their ordering, and a third tier with the idiomatic English translation. The words and their pronunciation might be recognisable to those familiar with French, but the ordering and spelling will be completely different.

(8)	*Bouki*	*vann*	*chat*	*la.*	
	Bouki	sell	cat	the	
	'Bouki sold the cat.'				
(9)	*Kolbè*	*fin(i)*	*devwa*	*li.*	
	Kolbè	finish	homework	third-person	
	'Kolbè has finished his homework.'				
(10)	*Mwen*	*fin*	*bati*	*kay*	*la.*
	First-person	finished	build	house	the
	'I have finished building the house.'				

The term **Creole** is shrouded in complicated ideology. Marginalised for not being 'proper languages' or deemed 'broken languages', many Creoles around the world are fighting against discrimination in a bid to gain linguistic recognition. To give just one example, despite the fact that 95% of Haitians are monolingual Kreyòl speakers, the education reforms of 1979 saw widespread opposition to the exclusive use of Haitian Creole in the first four years of schooling. Many parents – who were themselves monolingual – remain critical of these decisions. Some of the reasons cited include misplaced claims that Haitian Creole is a 'vulgar language', associated with 'the poor and the illiterate', as discovered by Wilson Douce (2023). This is sadly not an uncommon view of Creole languages.

On a more positive note, there are also some small gains in status and visibility for Haitian Creole. One of these comes from an announcement in the *Princetonian* newspaper that Kreyòl language courses are to be offered at its prestigious university beginning with 2025/2026 (Bernstein, 2024).

While Creole languages and by association, their speakers, have oftentimes been ridiculed and not taken seriously, there is another group of languages that has perhaps experienced even more prejudice: Pidgin languages.

Pidgins are languages that develop as a mode of communication between speakers who do not share a language – in other words, they develop in a very similar contact environment to Creoles. However, unlike Creoles, Pidgins do not function as the main language of their communities, with many (often most) community members remaining bilingual. By definition, pidgins are not acquired by children as a mother tongue, nor are they used in the home.

There are many Pidgins around the world: Nigerian Pidgin, Chinese Pidgin English, Aboriginal Pidgin English, Borgarmålet, Bombay Hindi, Français Tirailleur, Tsotsitaal and others. In fact, it is a myth to assume that Pidgins and Creoles are unusual or rare: we find such languages on every continent and for good reasons too (more on that in the next section). The APiCS Database mentioned earlier contains 76 Pidgins and Creoles alone, which is probably a highly conservative figure of the total number.

Here are two APiCS examples of Tok Pisin (Smith & Siegel, 2013). It does not take a trained linguist to recognise English as the lexifier language. The Indigenous Papuan language which provides the structure is Tolai. You will notice that Tolai has **inclusive pronouns**, like *yumi*, which mark explicitly whether the addressee is included or not. While in English, the first-person pronoun *we* is ambiguous between you-and-me and me-and-someone-else-but-not-you, in languages like Tolai, there are distinct forms which iron out this ambiguity by spelling out the exact meaning.

(11)	*Yumi*	*gat*	*ol*	*liklik*	*dok.*
	we-including-addressee	have	plural	small	dogs
	'We have little dogs.'				

(12)	*Tupela*	*pikinini*	*blongen*	*go*	*kisim*	*lip*	*banana.*
	Two-particle	child	belong-him	go	get	leaf	banana
	'His two children went to fetch banana leaves.'						

Although its name suggests Pidgin(-language) status, this classification is not without controversy. What may look like a neat and clear-cut distinction between Pidgins and Creoles on paper is difficult to apply in practice because speakers, languages and situations are messy and changeable. Thinking about Tok Pisin, a language that may have started out as a Pidgin, over time, it has clearly begun to shift towards a Creole, at least in certain areas. As Christine Jourdan (2021) explains, the pidgins of Papua New Guinea (*Tok Pisin*), the Solomon Islands (*Pijin*) and Vanuatu (*Bislama*) may all be second languages for many of their speakers, but they also constitute main community languages of large urban centres, and they are also mother tongues of two generations of urban speakers. So, should they be classed as Pidgins or Creoles? It depends on who you ask.

DRIVERS OF LANGUAGE CHANGE: VARIATION, CONTACT, PLAY

Not all changes that are observed in a language lead to such drastic outcomes as the creation of an entirely new language. Some changes are smaller, incremental and may even go completely unnoticed. As discussed in Chapter 5, every language involves a certain amount of variation, a general mass of in-flux choices that exist side by side, offering speakers options in how they express different ideas.

Despite our best efforts, it's impossible to accurately predict the changes that our language is likely to adopt in future, the shapes and forms giving rise to new ways of speaking. However, there are some corners of the system that we know to be more fluid and more open to change compared to others. In English, among these are **taboo** words, the quintessential 'bad words' (swear words), words expressing intensification like *very*, *lots*, *extremely* and a relatively unknown semantic corner known as vocatives.

If you know Latin or some other Romance language, you will know the **vocative case** as being a special grammatical form for calling out the addressee. More polite than *Oi!* and a grammatical add-on rather than a separate word. Or if you use social media, you might be familiar with the *@user* notation explicitly naming the addressee in a post or comment.

In spoken English, there are a series of words which do a similar job and which sort of look like vocatives. English does not use grammar (case) for it, but instead it uses lexis (words). These range from honorifics (*Madam, Sir*), to endearments (*honey, darling, cutie*), kinship terms (*mum, auntie, nan*) and even taboo words (*asshole, dick*). And like many other English words, these words have several functions, the vocative may be just one of them, so the context matters.

Compare (13) with (14) and (15) and note how different the use of the word *buddy* is in all three examples:

(13) Teacher to class: *Ok now pair up with a buddy and line up for assembly.*

(14) Father to son (following a bike accident): *You ok there, buddy?*
(15) Policeman to speeding driver: *OK buddy, get out of the car!*

In (13), it refers to a pairing, having a referential rather than a vocative function. In (14) and (15), on the other hand, it is used to address the listener (a vocative). Yet even as a vocative, *buddy* can have slightly different uses: as an empathetic marker in (14) showing compassion and as a commanding form in (15), subtly infused with a dose of camaraderie.

The term *buddy* is part of a coherent set of vocatives that function in similar albeit not identical ways. These include *dude, mate, bro, man* and *fella*. The vocative *man* (*Oh man, give it a rest already*!) has been around since Old English and is ubiquitous, whereas *buddy* is comparatively newer, coming into use in the nineteenth century, followed by the even more recent *dude*, which entered mainstream use in the 1960s (Needle & Tagliamonte, 2025, p. 127). *Bro* is the newest vocative on the block, along with a range of closely related variants *bruh, brah* and *bruv,* which have seen a meteoric rise in popularity with speakers born in the 2000s.

Alongside this trajectory of change, Jeremy Needle and Sali Tagliamonte (2025) describe how changes in vocative terms tell us something about changes in societal norms of gender construction. Here is how. These vocatives started life out as referential nouns (recall example 13), but over time, they got co-opted for adjacent though not unrelated functions, expressing solidarity, kinship and alignment. What is interesting is that this shift also led to a stripping of some of the referential properties they initially had. One such property is the reference to the male gender. As our own ideas about gender have become more fluid, so have perhaps our uses of male vocative terms.

As Needle and Tagliamonte illustrate from Canadian English interactions, speakers use terms like *man, dude* and *buddy* to refer to both men and women. Their data shows that not only are women using them to address other women (and men also use them to address women), but it is in fact women that drive this change: they are the innovators behind these uses. Moreover, this same pattern is not just a Canadian English peculiarity; it has been noted in other varieties of English, including British and Australian English.

Interestingly, not all change stabilises to become the new standard way of speaking. But when such change is perceived to be the new incoming standard, it is typically women who are the up-takers of change (Labov, 2001). This is not true just for vocatives, but it has been widely noted for many other language changes, from pronunciation to grammatical ones. And not just in English. For instance, Naomi Shin (2013) reviews cases of women leading language change in Pennsylvania German and Spanish, among others.

A further group of speakers who drive change is adolescents. Because of the many life changes which they are undergoing, young speakers are experimenting with all manner of symbolic resources: from dress to music and film preferences, all the way to vowel and lexical choices (Eckert, 1988). As with language in the big city, in a repertoire that is rich in variation and malleable to change – that of adolescents – innovation is rife.

These observations all point to the fact that a key ingredient in language change is variation. When there are multiple and closely related ways of saying similar things, one form may win over another, and over time, shifts in frequency of use can lead to changes in the whole system. In years to come, we might see *bro* completely wipe out the vocative use of *man*.

A second factor facilitating language change is language contact, that is, a mix of speakers from different linguistic communities, be they different dialects of the same language, or completely distinct and mutually unintelligible languages. Large urban centres accelerating the creation of new vernaculars and the hundreds of Pidgins and Creoles around the world are all testimony to the power of language contact.

Third and most fun of all is language play. In addition to transferring ideas and mitigating social relationships, we also use language for fun, to crack jokes, make puns, fool around and be creative. This is how we got **productive** (recurrent) uses of verbless chunks like [*Because* ____]: *Because life*, *Because language*, *Because grammar*. They are incomplete clauses and we can argue whether they are clauses at all, given they lack a verb, but that is beside the point. The point is that they deviate from standard English grammar and that they're used humorously to provide a highly relatable reason for a certain outcome. *Why do see these clauses? Because change.*

Another example is the similarly incomplete chunk [*I can't even*____], used to express exasperation or bewilderment. Figure 6.2 provides a caricatured version of the classic children's 1920s picture book *The little engine that could*, remixed into a modern version combining the start of the old title *The little engine that* followed by the much-frowned upon adverb *literally* (don't even get the prescriptivists started on this one), together with the incomplete phrase *can't even* (replacing the word *could* with *can't even*).

According to Marisa Brook and Emily Blamire (2023), language play is also the reason we will begin to see more nouns derived from adjectives through a process of **conversion** (literally, by doing nothing at all to the original form, see Chapter 2), *happy* instead of *happiness* in (16), *bitter* instead of *bitterness* in (17), *cute* instead of *cuteness* in (18), *awkwardness* instead of *awkward* in (19). Back in 2006, Justin

Figure 6.2 Literally, I can't even

Source: Know Your Meme – https://knowyourmeme.com/memes/literally

Timberlake thought he was *bringin' sexy back* but really, he might have just been bringing it in to begin with. And apparently, it's here to stay.

(16) Choose happ
(17) My bitter has been used up
(18) My voice changes when I see cute
(19) All it does is create 15 seconds of awkward

It is also how we have come to form words with the initials *Mc* in order to associate something with fast and cheap consumerism linked to McDonald's culture: *McMuffin, McCoffee, McNuggets, McWine, McGenius* and *McMansion.*

Language play also shows up in the form of creative spellings. Sometimes, these are used in certain online platforms, not just for the purpose of entertainment but also for evading censorship. Trolling through TikTok posts, Kendra Calhoun and Alexia Fawcett (2023) identified various examples created by users to avoid being banned for posting sensitive or prohibited material: *smoke weed* became *woke smeed*, *circumcised* became *sir-come-sized*, *sex* was *sects*, *sex worker* became *accountant*, leg booty was used instead of *LGBT*, *homophonic* instead of *homophobic* and *spicy eggplant* stood for *vibrator*. They call this repertoire **avoidance register**, a way of speaking which avoids unwanted attention, allowing the freedom to communicate about concepts and ideas that would otherwise be forbidden.

When the intention of keeping others in the dark goes beyond a few concepts, entire new languages can emerge. Termed **anti-languages**, these communication codes are deliberately devised to keep others in the dark. Well-known anti-languages include Pig Latin, a popular way of speaking devised by English-speaking children, Verlan, a French language of lower-class Parisians and Polari, the secret language of homosexual British men.

Change can arise from just about anything, from interactions between speakers who do not share a common language, to those wanting to deliberately keep others in the dark and those who just want to express their own unique identity in novel ways. But the mere presence of variation is not enough to bring about lasting change, sometimes it's here to stay, sometimes it's not. So, how can we know if something is going to stick?

BUT HOW DO WE KNOW?

As observed by Charles Darwin of biological evolution, language can be characterised by a similar process of descent with modification: language is passed on from generation to generation, but changes are introduced in the process.

Children learn their first language from their parents, but the transfer is not perfect; they do not speak exactly in the same way as their parents do, but in similar ways (more on that in Chapter 7). At the same time, the language they acquire is characterised by a certain amount of variation, contact and play, all of which can influence the pool of features present in a given language at any one time.

The picture is complicated by the fact that some of the variation remains stable across time, without one variant becoming more popular and pushing the other competing variants out. For instance, in English, verbs like *swimming*, *acting* and *breathing* are sometimes pronounced with an -IN sound at the end, and sometimes with a sound like -ING, close enough but not entirely the same one. Both forms have been around for some time and are used by different speakers in different contexts. The point is that there is no indication the variation is going to disappear anytime soon. For over 60 years, this one feature has been scrutinised intensely to better understand how speakers vary and why.

But other variants are not stable. They can sweep through the language, some quickly, some slowly, and obliterate all other competing forms, so that we are only left with one dominant feature reigning supreme over all others. Staying with English (only for simplicity), one such change was the move towards a single second-person pronoun *you*, and away from the two-form system *ye* and *you*. This shift took place during the sixteenth century (Sankoff, 2018).

A further change, which stabilised in the nineteenth century, is the transition to using the **present progressive** in sentences like *it is raining* or *I am writing* instead of the **simple present** *it rains* or *I write*, when expressing ongoing events (also discussed by Sankoff, 2018 in her review article).

We know all this from a collection of personal letters gathered in the *Corpus of Early English Correspondence* compiled by a team of Finnish researchers, who collected over 17,000 letters written by more than 2,000 people born between the 1400s and late 1600s. These letters have enabled us to piece together a comprehensive picture of language change throughout Modern English.

This may sound impressive (and it is), but historical linguists who study sound changes over thousands of years of change, track language change over even longer stretches of our history. Using known sound change rules, they have uncovered the fact that Proto-Indo-European probably had a word for *mother* that was something like **méhtēr*, not completely unrelated to the English word we still use today (in historical linguistics texts, the asterisk is used to denote a hypothesised form of the word, our best guess). Proto-Indo-European is approximately 7,000–8,000 years old and is the language that gave rise to the Indo-European languages spoken in parts of (modern) Europe and Southeast Asia today.

So how do we go about studying language change in the first place, given how many factors are at play? The most practical but least reliable way to investigate language change is by simulating the passing of time, through what we call **apparent time** research. This kind of work probes the language of speakers from the same community, but targets speakers of different age groups.

The vocative study is one example of an apparent time study. The drawback is that we do not know if the vocative patterns observed are changes linked to the speakers' stage of life (young speakers may just speak differently from older speakers) or whether we are really seeing a change-in-progress about to overhaul the entire system.

A more reliable way of investigating language change is by following a group of speakers around for many years and recording samples of their language at regular intervals (**panel study**). While valuable, these studies are notoriously difficult to pull off because participants get busy, move away and even die, making regular sampling of their language nearly impossible.

The data from the *Corpus of Early English Correspondence* is a rare gem because it allows precisely this kind of analysis, tracing the language of the same letter-writers throughout their lifetime.

A compromise might be to sample speakers from the same community at regular intervals but not always target the exact same individuals. This kind of study (**trend study**) is still done in real time but allows more flexibility.

In contrast to apparent time studies, both panel studies and trend studies necessitate the real passing of time, in other words, they take a long time to conduct. In the age of three-year-research-grants and publish-or-perish culture of today's university, such studies may be especially difficult to come by. Perhaps the age of social media will alleviate this problem in some small way by enabling panel studies to take place in a more practical manner: just download the entire history of avid users over their lifetime and there's your ready-made sample. Whatever the future holds for those studying language change, one thing we can be sure of: language is and continues to be on the move.

WANT MORE?

- Read Paul Kerswill and Heike Weise's 2022 book *Urban Contact Dialects and Language.*
- Watch Alex Gendler's Ted Ed Lesson "How languages evolve" (https://ed.ted.com/lessons/how-languages-evolve-alex-gendler).
- Play around with the fascinating online APiCS database (https://apics-online.info/).

7

LANGUAGE IN THE BRAIN

Although we sometimes claim to be speaking *from the heart*, it might make more sense to say we are speaking *from the brain*. The brain is the most important organ involved in language. Evidently, we need various other organs to produce and hear language, like facial muscles to articulate sounds, hands to produce signs and gestures, eardrums to hear sounds and so on, but the linguistic headquarters reside in the brain. This chapter unpacks various connections between language and the brain, beginning with how we learn our first language, then thinking about the multilingual brain and fast forwarding to the ageing brain.

LEARNING YOUR (FIRST) LANGUAGE

Children begin to learn language (**language acquisition**) well before they are born. Doting soon-to-be-parents who read to the 'bump' are not as crazy as they look. We now know the typical foetus begins to distinguish between different **vowel** sounds as early as 35 weeks after conception (Ibbotson, 2022, pp. 18–19). Vowels like A and E are the loudest sounds we make, produced with little obstruction of the air which means we can hold them for longer durations too (that's why we sing vowels and not consonants). Crucially, they are loud enough to be audible inside the womb.

During this time, the unborn foetus also learns to distinguish further phonetic characteristics, such as **tones** in languages that have these contrasts, like Mandarin, Thai, Zulu and Yoruba, **vowel duration**, again, in languages that use them, like Finnish, Māori, Japanese,

DOI: 10.4324/9781003621485-7

Czech and Hungarian and other phonological information relevant to the language(s) they are about to learn. These include the placement of **stress,** special emphasis that occurs in certain parts of words, and **intonation** patterns and the rise and fall patterns of connected speech (Ibbotson, 2022).

Although newborns can't name the languages they are learning, they are certainly already attuned to some of their characteristics by the time they come into the world. And what is more, they also show visible preferences for their own language over those of others (Clark, 2016, p. 68). How do we know this if they can't tell us explicitly? We can deduce their preferences by monitoring changes in sucking intensity, eye gaze and head-turning, the dilation of pupils and general brain activation.

The holy grail of language acquisition is not about what babies acquire or when but about sorting out how much innate linguistic knowledge they are born with versus how much they acquire from their immediate environment. This nature <—> nurture debate remains hotly contested between nativists, like Steven Pinker and cognitivists, like Michael Tomasselo.

A typical 9-month-old infant will have already formed an idea of their own language, culture and ethnicity. As Paul Ibbotson explains in his book on *Language Acquisition*, this knowledge arises from an ongoing process of **perceptual narrowing**, which cues infants to pay extra attention to those contrasts that they are regularly exposed to and ignore less relevant ones. For example, some languages make a contrast between sounds D and T (i.e., English, Japanese) while others don't (Yingkarta and Passamaquoddy) and children learn to weigh in (or not) on this and similar contrasts depending on whether their language has them.

While in principle, newborns retain the ability to distinguish a wide variety of sounds and phonetic properties well into their life outside the womb, perceptual narrowing leads them to lose this ability somewhere between 6 months and 12 months. In a nutshell, perceptual narrowing allows them to focus on what is specifically required in their mother tongue(s). Just imagine, by 12 months you have already reduced the capacity of your linguistic brain.

This means that throughout human development, we enter certain **critical windows** during which our brains are geared up to acquire certain information. After all, it's cognitively taxing to keep your brain (and ears) attuned to all possible sound contrasts of the 7,000 languages in existence. Not to mention inefficient given that you will likely only need the sounds found in (at most) a handful of languages. Perceptual narrowing is therefore an evolutionary process of optimising the work and effort needed from our brains.

While this mechanism is very clever, it does mean that we cannot afford to miss certain critical windows of development. Sure, the changes are not insurmountable, but they do get progressively harder to overcome as we age. Although we can learn languages later in life, no one claims it is easy.

Critical windows are discoverable in various ways. For example, recent studies investigating the effects of introducing screens early in an infant's life have uncovered grave concerns. Exposure to TVs and other screens in the first 12 months (or prior to the first word) is correlated with delayed language learning, and these effects are accentuated with prolonged exposure, say two hours or more per day (Massaroni et al., 2023). Passively watching a 'talking screen' with little or no feedback does not provide opportunities to fine-tune communication skills and misses a critical window of development. There are ways to mitigate these effects, like having the infant watch together with a parent or carer who is interacting with them while watching.

Depending on the family environment in which infants are socialised, they may grow up to become **monolinguals**, learning one language, **bilinguals**, learning two languages or **multilinguals**, learning three or more. Bilingualism (or multilingualism) can look very different depending on the circumstances and timing of how and when the various languages are introduced. Multilingualism has attracted both fascination and controversy, and there are several frustratingly persistent myths that endure in relation to it, some of which I will attempt to dispel in the next section.

Let's return to the first few weeks of an infant's life. For parents of newborns, this time seems ridiculously busy and at the same time agonisingly slow, filled with never-ending sleeping and feeding cycles. It might appear that not much else is going on but nothing could be further from the truth. During their first few weeks of life, infants already begin to engage in some early language production, even if we may not recognise it as such. They start making sucking noises, crying, cooing (at about six weeks), laughing (by 16 weeks) and other vocal play. Play is a key ingredient of language learning and language in general. These activities are acts of communication.

From about two or three months of age, infants form expectations regarding turn-taking, something that we adults take for granted. They grasp the idea that when people speak to one another, there is a recurrent pattern, one person speaks, then the other, and then perhaps the next. There is a normal pause that occurs between turns and sometimes overlapping speech can also occur. Experiments with young infants tell us that they will show surprise or even distress if this expectation is not met. Interestingly, experiments also show that while turn-taking patterns can vary across languages, the typical normal pause between turns remains astoundingly stable cross-linguistically (Ibbotson, 2022, p. 31).

From six months on, we can expect to hear **babbling**. These combinations of sounds, BABABABA, GAGAGA and DADADA, consist of consonant-vowel or vowel-consonant segments. Babbling is not just random language play, and like other language acquisition phenomena, babbling becomes increasingly specialised over time. We find that infants trying to acquire English babble their vowels along the kinds of patterns found in English, French learning infants produce more French-like vowels, for instance more nasalised versions, Cantonese infants babble with lower vowels and so on (Ibbotson, 2022, p. 47).

Between 9 months and 12 months, a huge cognitive leap occurs: infants begin to use pointing and gestures; they might point to a toy out of reach or an empty glass. They also begin to wave hello and goodbye. Deaf babies raised in speaking families, with little or no access to language input (Signed or otherwise) also begin to develop these skills around the same time. The deliberate harnessing of joint attention to make a point or to direct someone else to do something, maybe fill that empty glass with milk, or bring you the toy out of reach, albeit without actual words, represents an important milestone paving the way towards language.

At around 12 months, we begin to hear the first recognisable words. Initially, these are words that occur in isolation and denote precisely the things you might expect, often concrete (not abstract) entities, and things and people that infants are likely to encounter in their everyday interactions. Eve Clark (2016, p. 89) provides some examples of words that an English-speaking infant might begin to utter at this time, words for people (*daddy, mummy, baby, grandma*), food and drink items (*banana, juice, apple*), body parts (*nose, eye, hand*), clothing (*shoe, sock*), animals (*dog, kitty*), toys (*ball, book, ship*) and routinely used formulae (*hi, no, yes, night-night, peekaboo, thank-you, bye-bye*).

You might wonder about phrases like *thank-you*, why class them as words and not phrases? Initially, children treat chunks as single words, *baby-sleepy*, *mummy-sleepy*, *daddy-sleepy* and only later begin to segment word boundaries. This first stage, called the **one-word stage**, involves learning and using words as well as groups of words as though they were single words.

One lingering debate in this area relates to the necessity and usefulness of **Motherese**, that is, the simplified speech used by carers (often mothers) with their infants such as exaggerating their intonation, replacing certain lexical items like *rabbit* and *dog* with *bunny* and *doggy*, simplifying the structure and length of their phrases. Does adapting speech in this way lead to greater linguistic success? It's difficult to get a definitive answer to this question, but certainly engaging infants in natural conversation and addressing them directly seems to speed up the pace of acquisition. That said, ultimately, differences in cross-linguistic practices show that all children eventually catch up if they are exposed to language by puberty.

Having arrived at words, an infant's vocabulary increases exponentially. By two years, they will produce between 100–600 distinct words, by six years, they can understand around 14,000 words and produce slightly fewer (Clark, 2016, p. 87). How we count words (see Chapter 2) influences the numbers greatly, the point is not to give a precise idea of the actual word count but to note that the count increases rapidly. Production lags behind comprehension, which also explains why young infants can understand much more than they can say.

I should also add that these counts vary considerably between families, social groups and cultures. Some American children are exposed to 600 words per hour, others to as many as 2100 words. Extrapolating these counts over four to five years, researchers have come up with a rather alarming-sounding **30-million-word-gap** between children. Now, this gap correlates with various social factors, such as education, social status and income. While some have actively championed to redress this inequality, think Obama's 2014 *Bridging the Word Gap* initiative, others have been more cautious and sceptical of the figures, pointing out various flaws with the calculations made. Be that as it may, one thing that everyone seems to agree on is that engagement with young infants leads to positive outcomes.

Returning to the one-word stage, this is a phase of lexical expansion but also one characterised by various changes in how words are said and used. First, let's look at **phonological** (sound) adjustments. Because pronouncing words can be tricky, requiring fine-grained control of articulators, infants resort to various adjustments to make it easier (Clark, 2016, pp. 121–123). Some sounds get substituted for others: *pie* might sound like BAI where a P sound would be replaced by a B sound, *soon* might sound like DUN, replacing the more difficult sound S with an easier one D, and *rabbit* may come out as WAABIT, replacing the tricky R sound with the easier W. And if it's all hard, just leave it out altogether: *banana* becomes NANA, *slide* becomes LIDE and *milk* becomes MIK. Other sounds get copied (or reduplicated): *bottle* becomes BABA, *daddy* becomes DADA and *blanket* might be BABI.

Conversely, if you've worked hard enough to learn a particular word, why not make the most of it and use it lots? **Overextending** words is a way of using a given word for a wider or more general meaning than it's typically used (Clark, 2016, pp. 95–96). For example, the word *dog* might be used to refer to other four-legged animals like cats, sheep and horses. Or *ball* might be used to refer to any other round object, like lamps, apples and oranges as well as doorknobs and pieces of soap. Don't be fooled by the English examples, children learning other languages engage in this phenomenon too. Overextension might affect as much as 40% of a one-to-two-year-old's vocabulary. But if this is your child, fear not, they sort out the meanings eventually. And the same goes for incorrect grammatical forms, like the over-regularisation of past tense verbs: *bring-bringed, see-seed, give-gived*.

Slowly, the one-word stage gives way to the **multi-word stage**, an exciting time when children stand at the gateway of novel language production. Citing work by Michael Tomasello, Eve Clark (2016, Table 7.10, p. 199) provides the following sequence, evidencing the transition from one-word stage to multi-word stage in the context of spilling something. The examples beautifully demonstrate the cognitive leaps that the infant is making in expanding their speech repertoire.

Age	Utterance
1y 7m	*spilled-it*
	spilled-it a beard [spilled juice on chin]
	mommy spilled-it on leg [telling mother about spill]
	spill-it couch [spilled juice on couch]
	spill-it leg [telling father about spill]
	spill-it table...made-this...spill this...fall-down [telling someone about spilling juice]
	spill-it tummy [telling father about spill]
1y 9m	*I never will spill-it* [after being warned not to spill drink]
	spilled wheezer milk [spilt cat's milk]
1y 10m	*spill something over mommy's coat* [sees stain on mother's coat]
1y 11m	*I spilled it* [did so, twice]
	I spilled the blackboard [??]
	won't spill it anymore [promise]

To begin with, *spilled-it* starts out as a frozen chunk, it might as well be a single word. Gradually, it becomes inserted inside other constructions, like *mommy spilled-it on leg*, and while it's still uttered without a pause between the two words involved, we can gradually see a shift towards an awareness of its internal structure. Over time, the past tense *-ed* marker drops out, turning the 'word' from *spilled-it* to *spill-it*. Next, the increase in scenarios and contexts expands to spillages on the couch, on the leg, on the tummy and as the saying goes, practice does make perfect because eventually, the chunk becomes *spilled* and *it* gets dropped altogether (*spilled wheezer milk*). By two years of age, the infant figures out that the word is (just) *spill* and that its shape can be modified depending on the timing of the event (present *spill*, past *spilled*).

This iterative process provides the building blocks for how language is acquired. Although there is still so much more left for our infant to learn about words and patterns (grammar), and about meanings and associations, by the time their fourth or fifth birthday comes around, they attain a rather sophisticated grasp of the nuts and bolts of language.

However, there is still more to acquire even at this point. Sometime between 8 and 11 years, children begin to orient themselves more to their peers than their parents and carers, acquiring information about what is cool and trendy, which accents are valued, which words make you sound old or how boys and girls talk differently from each other. All this social information, so important and yet implicitly communicated, is also a crucial part of language acquisition.

THE MULTILINGUAL BRAIN

This process is all well and good if we assume a **monolingual** view of the world, in which infants learn only one language to begin with. However, monolingualism is hardly representative of reality for most of us. The fact is that there are more bilingual or multilingual people in the world than there are monolinguals.

When multiple languages are in play, life can look very different depending on how and when the various languages are introduced in the life of the individual. Let's stick with two languages for simplicity while keeping in mind that the distinctions discussed apply equally to multiple languages. Bilinguals are likely to fall into one of the following three types: some learn two languages simultaneously from birth (or close to it, roughly before the age of three) being **compound bilinguals**. Others learn one language to begin with but add another relatively early on, typically in a different context, say at school, while continuing their **heritage language** at home. These are **coordinate bilinguals**. The third type are **subordinate bilinguals**, they add a second language later in life, after puberty and learn it through the means of their first, translating from one language into another.

Note that these distinctions contrast not just in terms of the age when a second language might be introduced, but also the context in which it is added, say home versus school. These ideas were first formulated in the 1960s by Eric Lenneberg under the **Critical Period Hypothesis** (CPH).

According to Lenneberg, a critical period takes place between two years of age and somewhere around puberty, you can think of it is a wide critical window, which predisposes the infant brain towards automatic language learning. In Lenneberg's own words

(1967, p. 176, cited by Norrman, 2024, p. 2) "automatic acquisition from mere exposure to a given language seems to disappear after this age, and foreign languages have to be taught and learned through a conscious and labored effort". What is more "foreign accents cannot be overcome easily after puberty".

It's a matter of great debate whether a foreign **accent** is a good or a bad thing and I will return to this shortly, but two observations are in order first. One is that merely exposing a young infant to a second/foreign language in a passive manner will not result in a proficient bilingual. Experiments back in the 1970s investigated the effects of technology on multilingualism, showing that putting say, a Dutch-speaking child in front of German language TV, in this case, *Sesame Street*, will not render them bilingual (Clark, 2016, p. 46). This should not come as a surprise given the importance of feedback and joint attention in language acquisition.

Second, even for those of us that do end up being proficient bilinguals, at whatever age, the matter is not settled once and for all, remaining constant throughout our lives. Bilingualism is not a stable quality but an ever-changing and frustratingly transient variable. Some of us lose our first language. Some of us gain second or third language(s) and then go on to lose them later in life. Languages, like the plants in your garden, require constant attention and tender loving care: maintenance (Figure 7.1). **Language maintenance** is an active field and the core business of many language planning committees and various government bodies who regulate and legislate language use.

The Swiss linguist François Grosjean describes the reality of bilingualism in insightful detail in his 2010 book *Bilingual: life and reality*. He also dispels many myths associated with being bilingual. One myth relates to the idea that bilinguals are two monolinguals in one body (Figure 7.2). You might just think this is a fun metaphor, but this way of thinking has grave consequences for how we test, teach and think of bilinguals.

How do most people think of bilinguals? Many people understand them as perfect mini dictionaries, able to translate any statement from one language into another, switching between languages as you might switch between TV channels. But that's not how things work. Unless you are a rare individual or an experienced professional translator, bilingual lives look something like this: you

Figure 7.1 Languages require maintenance
Illustration credit Paul D. James

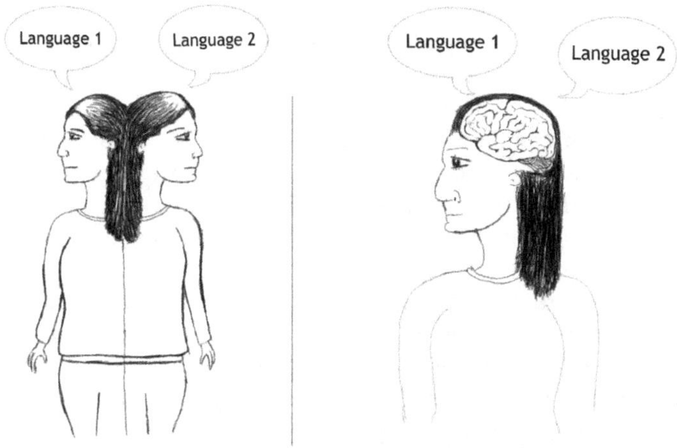

Figure 7.2 Bilingual brain: left panel – the myth, right panel – the reality
Illustration credit: Paul D. James

speak one language at home and another at work, maybe use bits of a third language in a neighbouring town during your weekly shop because it's cheaper there. Talking about work matters in your home language is agonisingly hard and vice versa. Different languages are associated with different situations and contexts.

What is more, languages are not neatly delineated entities that co-exist inside the same brain, they are constantly mixing, so that all our languages are activated every time we communicate. This is one reason why bilinguals experience interference from one language into another. As I am writing this chapter, I might listen to music containing French lyrics and so, the French-speaking part of my brain activates that language, even while my fingers are typing English language sentences. Walking past a billboard, watching a movie, scrolling through different social media posts – all of these activities keep our multilingual brains constantly on, foregrounding and backgrounding whichever language is needed.

Unsurprisingly, language mixing of this sort does not just stay within our brains, but it also happens out loud, while speaking (codeswitching) and it is perfectly normal. Counterintuitively perhaps, **codeswitching**, using bits from one language while speaking another, isn't a sign of language deficiency but rather of language proficiency. It's tempting to assume that bilinguals mix languages because they are unable to speak one language well enough. While that can sometimes happen when learners are beginning to find their words, for the great majority of bilinguals, codeswitching is purposeful mixing of languages either to highlight shared (linguistic) common ground with another speaker, or for symbolic reasons. For example, if I was relaying a conversation I had with my mother to another Romanian/English bilingual, I might use a mix of Romanian and English, relating the **direct speech** said using precisely the words that we each used.

Another problem arising from the two-monolinguals-in-one-body view is the assumption that a monolingual speaker represents the target of language proficiency. Imagine being asked to look at some pictures and then to express in your language what you see. If you are monolingual, say you speak language A, then you will express this in A. Now imagine a bilingual speaker being asked to express the same content in each of their languages (call them A and B), separately. Some language tests assume that what the monolingual speaker says constitutes the 'right' answer for language A. But what if the bilingual speaker does not express themselves in language A in the same way that the monolingual speaker did? My colleague Jeanine Treffers-Daller and I did this kind of study with French and English bilinguals of various levels of proficiency and found that experienced bilinguals differed in the way they expressed the events from *both* monolinguals and early language learners (Treffers-Daller & Calude, 2015). Bilinguals are just different people. They need to be tested with materials designed for them, not for monolinguals.

Monolinguals do not constitute an appropriate yardstick for evaluating bilinguals. Assessing any deviation from monolingual behaviour as a deficiency represents a completely misinformed view of how language works. And that includes children.

Decades ago, it used to be commonly thought that bilingualism was bad for children because bringing children up with multiple languages was deemed to lead to confusion and to smaller vocabularies, not to mention the apparently dreaded presence of codeswitching. Another misinformed view. If testing vocabulary sizes of bilingual children in one of their languages, then sure, they would perform worse than monolingual children in that (one) language. But adding together all the words that bilingual children acquired in both languages has consistently showed that bilingual children have larger (combined) vocabularies than monolingual children.

In fact, the bilingual brain must work incredibly hard to keep up. If you have ever tried learning another language, you will be familiar with foreign language dictionaries. Looking up the German word *Wald* in an English dictionary gives two different words *forest* and *wood*, in New Zealand English or Australian English, it might also give *bush*. In French, it will be *forêt* or *bois*, in Swahili *msitu* but also *nyika*.

Does this mean these words can be used interchangeably? Put another way, are they perfect **synonyms**? Not entirely. They have similar meanings but not identically overlapping ones. It all depends on the context in which they are used. These words are said to exhibit **multiple equivalence** (De Deyne et al., 2023), which means that one word (e.g. *Wald*) covers concepts that are expressed by different words in a different language (e.g. *forest*, *wood* or *bush*).

A related case involves partial overlap. The French verb *savoir* translates to *know* in English, but there's a catch: it cannot be used to refer to knowing people, only knowing things. Therefore, *savoir* covers a partial meaning of *know* because it specifically relates to knowing things (for people, there's a different verb: *connaître*). Similarly, Slavic languages have a single word covering what English encodes with two: a single word for *foot* and *leg*, one word meaning both *arm* and *hand*, *finger* and *toe*. Despite being a Romance language, Romanian is the same as Slavic in this respect: *picior* ('foot, leg'), *mână* ('hand, arm'), *deget* ('toe, finger').

Conversely, some words cannot be translated at all. It's not that you can't express those meanings in other languages but that you need whole phrases or even short sentences to express the same meaning. *Tingo* means 'to borrow things from a friend's house, one by one until there is nothing left' in the language spoken on Easter Island (De Boinod, 2007). In Chinese, *huiji-jiyi* means 'to avoid following your doctor's advice for fear of being recognised as the sufferer of a disease'. Malay has a word for the relationship between two brothers' wives or two sisters' husbands (*biras*), and Persian has one for a woman who hates her husband (*farik*). Although English has no direct (word-to-word) translation for any of these things, as you can see from above, we can express the same meaning, we just need more words to do it. This kind of phenomenon (**zero equivalence**) is always a favourite with speakers who seem to take pride in the fact that their language has a word with a meaning that is not lexicalised in other languages. Except for German speakers, who probably wish no one spread the *Schadenfreude* ('to take pleasure in another's misfortune') memes on the internet.

Cross-linguistic dictionaries imply the existence of one-to-one equivalence between words across languages. Danko Šipka (2019) set out to quantify this very thing about five years ago and found that even in languages from the same language family (Indo-European), like French, Spanish and Serbian, **full equivalence** was only found in a quarter of the dictionary entries. Most entries exhibited either partial or multiple equivalence. What this means for bilinguals is that they must remember not just the actual words found in their different languages, but also the specific idiosyncratic ways in which these forms carve up the world.

And beyond meanings, there is also the thorny issue of different ways of grouping words (grammar). For example, the English verb *write* occurs in phrases like *X wrote to Y* (*I wrote to him*). In German, there's no *to*, just *X wrote Y* (*Ich schrieb ihm*), Y carries a special marker to denote it as the receiver of the action. In Swahili, everything is crammed into a single word *nilimwandikia* 'I-wrote-to-him' (see Chapter 2 for more on words and Chapter 3 for more on grammar).

LANGUAGE THROUGH THE LINGUISTIC BRAIN

The bilingual brain is not just impressive in its abilities to juggle multiple languages, but it is can also exhibit some unexpected additional benefits. One of these is the **Foreign Language Effect**.

In a series of well-replicated experiments, researchers have uncovered that bilinguals reason differently in their native language than they do in their (later acquired) second languages. This makes sense because everything is harder in a second language. But here is the unexpected bit: because bilinguals reason more slowly and less automatically in their additional language(s), their decisions rely less on knee-jerk reactions and emotional triggers and more on deliberate and explicit reasoning processes. If you are a fan of the Nobel prize winner Daniel Kahneman and his 2011 book *Thinking, fast and slow*, this is the 'thinking slow' bit. And sometimes, that can lead to more logical outcomes. This is commonly referred to as the Foreign Language Effect (Dylman & Champoux-Larsson, 2020).

If you were expecting the Foreign Language Effect to denote some kind of bias that people generally hold against non-native speakers, you would not be completely barking up the wrong tree (in case you are wondering, translating this idiomatic saying into Romanian word by word makes little sense, we would prefer to say *a te certa cu fantoma* 'to argue with a ghost'). Such a bias definitely exists, and it extends well beyond English (accents) and adult stereotypes. Children orient themselves towards native accents more than non-native ones. For example, already by 10–12 months old, they will be more likely to accept a toy from a native-accented speaker than a foreign-accented one (DeJesus et al., 2022). Non-native speaking adults are influenced in how they see themselves also: those who exhibit stronger accents in their second language report lower levels of belonging within their second-language communities (Gluszek & Dovidio, 2010).

There are many fascinating avenues to consider when we peer inside our linguistic brains. I will content with one more example here, namely one which relates to a pressing concern in our current modern world: truth and misinformation. It turns out that our brains are excellent sponges for absorbing implicit frequencies with which a certain event has occurred. Not only that, but we are also impressively and worryingly suggestive creatures too. Before you rush into thinking this is a good thing, let me show you some downsides.

No matter how incorrect a statement might be, if we hear it often enough, we eventually begin to believe it's true. Even exposing people to a given topic without an associated assertion (*The elephant enclosure*) can later affect their predisposition to believe that a related statement is true (*Elephants need less space to survive than zebras*). And you guessed it: the language used matters also! If the same (relatively fixed) combination of words is used each time, that immediately increases our gullibility too (Zhang & Schwarz, 2020). This happens because our brains like easy tasks: being able to parse language we have already encountered is cognitively less taxing; something called **fluency**. Recall the bottleneck-of-attention in Chapter 1 and add to that all the things we need to do each day, millions of tasks, the constant rush of information thrown at us, scrolling through endless emails, can you blame our poor brains for wanting to take shortcuts? Perceived truth heavily leans on fluency, which predisposes our brains to believe that which they can easily understand, the familiar, … because if it's clear and recognisable, then it's probably true, right!?

But it gets worse. Our memories are also highly influenceable and suggestive. Eye-witness experiments show that testimony can change simply as a result of even the smallest tweaks in the words used to interrogate a witness in court (Loftus & Zanni, 1975). Compare these sentences:

(1) Did you see a broken headlight?
(2) Did you see the broken headlight?

Did you spot the difference between them? It's so subtle, yet so significant. The indefinite article *a* is used in (1) and the definite article *the* in (2). Grammatically speaking, the definite article implies specificity (*there was a headlight and it was broken*), whereas the indefinite article is more uncertain (*a possible broken headlight*). And so, led astray by grammar, the second sentence is statistically more likely to lead to a recollection of a broken headlight compared to the first sentence (Loftus & Zani, 1975). But that's just grammar and not memory.

LANGUAGE IN THE AGEING BRAIN

Fast forward to the end of our lives, what happens as we age and what effect does our ageing brain have on language? The link between language, brain and health has been established since at least the nineteenth century, when Pierre Paul Broca identified the left hemisphere as housing a part of the brain that is largely responsible for handling language (Broca's area). Like Carl Wernicke, Broca and many of the early scholars working on language and gerontology approached it from a pathological perspective, which is to say looking at what happens when things start to go wrong. Early scholars wanted to know what goes wrong and how this impacts communication.

Indeed, older adults tend to experience much frustrating and inevitable decline, see some examples in Figure 7.3. Many of the effects described in the table arise in ageing (but otherwise

Word finding failures

- being unable to recall proper nouns (*John, Jacinda, Austria*) happens earlier than difficulty in retrieving common nouns (*table, book, love*)

T(ip)-O(f)-T(ongue) events

- wanting to utter a known word but being unable to do so

Spelling errors

- misspelling common and previously known words

Disfluencies

- using more fillers like *you know*, more *umms* and longer pauses

Syntactic simplification

- simplying phrases and using more formulaic chunks

Narrative structure changes

- going on tangents and making off-topic remarks, more repetitions

Figure 7.3 Changes observed in language use as we age

non-pathological) adults. However, these issues are amplified in individuals affected by dementia and other similar conditions.

But the news is not all grim. Research also tells us that while indeed vocabulary represents the first part of the language system to be affected by cognitive decline, ahead of sounds (phonology) and structure (grammar), it is also words that provide some good news. Older adults have larger vocabularies compared to young adults and more experience in communicating with others (admittedly, this will vary greatly from individual to individual). And this experience can help mitigate some of the changes mentioned in Figure 7.3. For instance, older adults will engage in various strategies of **repair** counteracting their inability to retrieve a word or piece of information that's being asked of them. Here is a transcript of a conversation between a Chinese (Alzheimer's) patient and their doctor (Chen et al., 2024, p. 129):

(3) DOC: *Jintian xingqi ji*
What day is today
[pause]
PAT: *Jintian xingqi ji a*
What day is today ah
DOC: *En-*
Hm-
PAT: *-na wo ye meiji zhe*
-I don't remember that either
DOC: *En hehe*
Hm hehe
PAT: *Yinwei zhege dongxi wo bushi wo you bushangke you bugan shenme*
Because of this I am not I don't have classes and I don't do anything
DOC: *-Aiya dui dui dui*
-Well right right right

The patient is clearly struggling to provide answers to the doctor's questions. But rather than not saying anything at all and shutting down the interaction, they first repeat the doctor's question (*Jintian xingqi ji a* 'What day is today ah'), and then after admitting they don't know the answer, go on to use another repair strategy: supplementing the lack of knowledge with an excuse justifying their gap (*Yinwei zhege dongxi wo bushi wo you bushangke you bugan shenme* 'Because of this I am not I don't have classes and I don't do anything').

It's no secret that we are all getting older. By 2050, 15.6% of the world's population is predicted to be over 65 and by 2100, that number is set to increase to 24% (Song, 2024, p. 169). So, it's important to go beyond merely documenting the effects of the ageing brain and to also consider ways of improving the lived experience of older people. Indeed, the last 20–30 years have seen a shift from pathological approaches to language in old age, towards a focus on better palliative care, improved targeted interventions and practical advice for those affected by cognitive decline.

So, what have we learnt? Language really does seem to be a use-it-or-lose-it skill. Loneliness is not just bad for our bodies but also for our language. Engagement in daily conversations keeps our white cells intact and our grey cells' density (Huang & Boyd, 2024). Increasing linguistic practice and familiarity leads to higher fluency, reduced tip-of-tongue events, and higher word retrieval ability. Perhaps the 30-million-word-gap might suitably apply to older adults as it does to young infants.

One factor in all these undesirable effects experienced by older adults is the inescapable fact that language relies on multiple senses, especially the ability to hear (for speaking and listening) and see (for reading). Background noise, poor hearing and poor eyesight interfere with linguistic production and with the motivation to engage in language exchange in the first place.

Paralleling Motherese (the adapted speech used by carers with infants), we can speak of a way of adapting language in order to facilitate interactions with older speakers: **Elderspeak**. Elderspeak involves slowing down the speech rate, speaking louder, repetitions, elaborations to facilitate retrieval, simplifying complexity of structures or shortening phrases (Burke & Shafto, 2011). Is it helpful? Some adjustments are helpful, such as simplifying phrases, while others are not, like speaking louder in a more exaggerated voice. It could also be that obvious changes lead the older adult for whose benefit they are performed to feel stupid and patronised, which decreases their satisfaction with the interaction. Ultimately, different adaptations work for different individuals.

And what of multilingual older brains? It does seem that speaking multiple languages can offer protection against cognitive decline, or at the very least a delay in the onset of dementia and similar diseases (Kim et al., 2019). Moreover, the protection increases with the number of languages spoken.

Can you get this extra layer of protection later in life, say after the age of 60 or 70, or is it too late by then? The jury is still out on this one, with some studies reporting an increase in brain plasticity following as few as three months of intensive language learning, while others not being able to identify statistically significant improvements (Wei et al., 2024). One thing is clear: learning another language, at any age, leads to further opportunities for social interaction, a decrease in loneliness and a general increase in a sense of self-worth and personal growth, so it's best to give it a go anyway. *Ciao tutti*!

WANT MORE?

- Read Paul Ibbotson's *Language: The Basics* (2022).
- Watch Mia Nacamulli's TedEd Lesson "The benefits of the multilingual brain" (https://www.youtube.com/watch?v=MMmOLN5zBLY).
- Check out Adam Jacot de Boinod's book *The Meaning of Tingo* (2007) for amusing and fascinating words from around the world.

8

LANGUAGE AND COMPUTERS

"It seems as though everything happens faster on the internet" writes Adam Aleksic in his 2025 book *Algospeak* (p. 37). And he ought to know because he makes a living from his influencer content on TikTok, Instagram and YouTube. So much of our communication happens across fibre optic wires these days. Moreover, a whole lot of communication takes place via machines and automated tools.

From mobile phones, to chatbots and ChatGPT, our modern world has us increasingly 'talking' with machines. Siri can play our chosen music; Google translates foreign language reviews and Alexa will search for that perfect gift. But is all that really 'talking'?

Such computational tools can parse language, produce it and summarise it. We also use them to analyse large collections (**corpora**) of language to better understand how language works in the first place. And it seems that machine learning algorithms used on social media are not just learning our habits and preferences but are also ramping up language change by driving a high turnover of new words and phrases.

As I am writing this chapter, it's daunting to realise that it will already be out of date by the time it is sent to the publisher, let alone read by you, the reader. Nowhere is the pace of modern life felt more acutely than in the realm of technology. More, faster, now. These tenets are responsible for a huge acceleration in the way we live today. With that in mind, my goal is not to present the latest and most up-to-date computational tools available but instead, to provide an overview of the main areas in which computers have had and continue to have a major influence in how we use and understand language.

DOI: 10.4324/9781003621485-8

CAN MACHINES COMMUNICATE?

In a landscape peppered with virtual assistants and chatbots, it has become commonplace to talk about machines 'learning' to perform tasks, including 'speaking' with us. But are they really learning anything and is this actual communication?

History gives us two major contrasting approaches to communication. One approach sees communication as the transmission of information. This is the central idea of a theory proposed by Claude Shannon in the late 1940s. Shannon eventually formalised his idea into what we now call the **mathematical theory of communication.** The 1948 article in which he laid out his theory is thought to be one of the most cited scientific papers of all time. Incidentally, in the same article, he also introduced the computational term 'bit'. Coming back to communication, adopting Shannon's view sees communication heavily tied in with information, the referential content being conveyed.

A different approach was proposed by James William Carey some 50 years later. This focuses on the **ritual view of communication.** For Carey, communication is all about ritualised and organised means of sharing information, emphasising the social aspect of the process rather than the information per se.

Carey wrote a book on the subject in 1989, *Communication as Culture*, which examines the history and impact of the telegraph. The telegraph – back then an amazing technological feat, but something we now see as an archaic relic of the past – went on to revolutionise the transmission of information across physical space. For the first time ever, people could communicate with others across the world, instantly. Language could now be transported and in that process, humanity began to witness a separation between communication and transmission, two processes that were previously inseparable. How commonplace this seems today, but what a revolutionary notion back then (Figure 8.1).

These ideas about the function and nature of communication are still relevant today, even though the telegraph itself is not. Social media and increased globalisation have made it possible for more people to connect across the globe than ever before. And as we saw in Chapter 4 in the discussion of deictics, *here* and *now* can mean wildly different things in different interactions.

Figure 8.1 A telegraph used to transmit information via Morse code (reproduced under creative commons licence from Wikipedia)

Although both approaches to communication are valid, they capture different aspects of the process. Over time, the question has shifted from how has the use of technology influenced our communication to what happens when we begin to communicate with machines themselves?

In 1950, Alan Turing formulated the 'imitation game', now largely known as the Turing Test, in which an individual sends questions to a machine in one room and an individual in another room. But here's the catch: this individual does not know which is which. The goal of the 'game' is to tell apart machine from human, based on the answers received. Put another way, can the machine imitating a human cunningly pass itself as one without detection? Not only did Turing mean to use this test to see if machines could accurately communicate on a par with humans, but also as a test of intelligence: could machines think?

And for a long time, machines failed this test. We humans could smugly feel superior knowing that our said individual could successfully work out which answers came from another human and which were produced by a machine.

However, nowadays, this is no longer the case. The latest chatbots are making it impossible to tell machine generated answers apart from human replies thereby passing the Turing Test. More than a mere 'game', this has become a huge concern for educators trying to design assignments that are increasingly completed by the likes of ChatGPT instead of the students taking the course. And education is only one realm where machines imitating humans opens up a can of worms. More on this soon. Which brings us to artificial intelligence (AI). AI is so smart these days that we are beginning to believe our own metaphor that machines really do 'think'.

But not so fast, caution Emily Bender and her colleagues (Bender et al., 2021 and Bender & Hanna, 2025). In a much-cited 2021 article, they argue that machines are nothing short of *stochastic parrots* (they used this very phrase in the title of their paper); they do not 'understand', 'learn' or 'think' anything but simply repeat recombined and remixed human-produced utterances in a parroted-like fashion.

So, can machines communicate? The answer boils down to what we really mean by 'communicate'. The answer is 'yes', if what we want is to ask a question and receive an answer back. Conversely, the answer is 'no', if what we are after is a feeling entity that provides original answers, which are not remixed versions of previously produced speech. It is true that much of our own speech is also formulaic and prefabricated (see the section on spoken language in Chapter 1), but it comes through the filter of a sentient human mind with a breathing and feeling heart.

Be that as it may, regardless of what answer we decide on, it's undeniable that machines are used in several tasks that involve language, some of the major ones being: machine translation, natural language processing and virtual assistants.

MACHINE TRANSLATION

If you know your science fiction classics, you might be familiar with *Babel fish*, the quirky creation of Douglas Adams:

> The Babel fish … is small, yellow and leech-like, and probably the oddest thing in the Universe. …. …. if you stick a Babel fish in your ear you can instantly understand anything said to you in any form of language.
>
> [*The Hitch Hiker's guide to the Galaxy* by Douglas Adams, 1978, pp. 49–50]

The concept of Babel fish sounded incredible in 1978. Just imagine having an automatic translator being able to decode any message from any language into any language, straight into your ear. But how does it sound today? Nowhere near as impressive. And that's because we already have technology that can get us almost as close as Babel fish. It may not be small, yellow or leech-like, but it can translate things fast. It may not be perfectly accurate, but it gets us a long way there, and sometimes that's good enough.

Last year, as my family sat around the table of our rented apartment in the heart of Brussels, I watched my barely teenage children matter-of-factly swipe a page from their French textbook through Google Translate, on the iPad that their new school had lent them. The text instantly flashed from French into English. Not perfect. Not perfectly accurate. This was no Shakespeare mind, but it was sufficiently apt to translate the questions they were asked to answer about the novel everyone was reading in class. They could participate even though their French was rudimentary at best. Next, I watched them formulate answers in English and we discussed how we might go about translating these back into French for school. Nothing was stopping them from reversing the process to translate their English answers back into French, beyond their desire to improve their French. This level of participation in a new language would have taken me years, back when I switched from Romanian to English as a newly arrived immigrant teenager.

Translation tools are becoming part of our day-to-day reality. Whether we use them to quickly make sense of a post on social media written in a language we do not speak, or to get the gist of an online review to decide about a product or service; they're cheap, readily available and fast. We think nothing of it. However, using machines to automate translation only began about 70 years ago, in the advent of the Second World War.

Many say that the story of **machine translation** started with Warren Weaver. He was born in the late 1800s and went on to become a mathematician and scientist, but he also served in the Air Service during the First World War. Military ideas were at the forefront of many lives during that time, including his own, and having been exposed to cryptography and cybernetics, it wasn't a huge leap for Weaver to contemplate the use of 'calculating machines' for communication and translation purposes (Gunkel, 2025a, pp. 18–19).

In fact, when you think about it, cryptography is a kind of translation. Coding and decoding secret messages constitute just as much of a translation exercise as coding and decoding messages between any (human) languages, regardless of whether the person speaking (or writing) cares about someone else intercepting their communication. Secret languages (Chapter 6) like Polari, the secret code British gay men used to use in order to pass on messages to each other during a time when homosexuality could land you in jail, or Pig Latin, a game devised by children to communicate with each other, have been around for a long time, even though Google or Microsoft hasn't produced automatic translation tools for them.

Weaver died in 1978, at the age of 84, before highly accessible machine translation tools had permeated the world. But his vision that machines could be used to translate various codes is very much a reality, whether we are talking about made-up codes deliberately designed to keep others in the dark, or human languages unfamiliar to a given speaker.

How did machine translation techniques evolve over time? As David Gunkel explains in his book *AI for Communication*, classical machine translation initially started off as a collection of transformational rules, applied by leveraging computational speed. These rules are essentially repeated dictionary-look-up functions, designed to match strings, sometimes words, sometimes phrases from one language into another. This method is handy and often what second-language learners do as they begin to acquire the very basics of the language they are trying to learn. However, this sort of process quickly runs into trouble as structures match poorly across languages and the problem of 'that's just not how we say it in X-ish' [insert your language here] begins to render the exercise jarring and clumsy.

A second problem comes from the fact that attempting to build a universal translator from *any* language to *any* other language – a true Babel fish – becomes difficult, not to mention, slow and inefficient to implement using this design. One way around it to have a designed interlanguage which acts as the intermediary language into which and from which everything is translated.

In the 1980s, a new method emerged to get around some of these problems: example-based machine translation (Gunkel, 2025a, pp. 22–23). Considering English and Japanese translations, Makato Nagao recognised that bilinguals do not simply operate a dictionary-lookup function inside their heads when shifting between one language into another. Instead, they appear to translate on a more global level, from construction to construction, at the phrasal and sometimes, sentence level. So, Nagao set out to program machines to simulate precisely this process. By taking thousands of already (human-)translated texts, he designed a new way of automating translation. His method worked to some extent but as is often the case, it brought up its own problems, not least the requirement of thousands of existing high-quality translations between the languages in question.

Example-based machine translation was followed by statistical machine translation, which ultimately paved the way for machine learning translation. These methods use probabilistic models of word co-occurrence and associations between words – ranging from more or less sophistication – to estimate the most likely contender to follow a particular word or phrase.

Just to give a very simple example, if you have the word *bonsai*, you know with high certainty that the most likely word to follow will be *tree*. A corpus will immediately show you the probability of this, something our brains do not 'know' explicitly but according to some theories of language, they do 'know' implicitly through repeated exposure. Similarly, the word *herring* is very likely preceded by *red*, though of course, *red* can precede many different other words as well. **Word collocations** need not be bidirectional; words do not mutually attract one another, the pull can be stronger from one word to another word, but not the other way around.

More abstractly, you have whole formulae like *what's this X doing in my Y* which is a ready-made chunk that our brains instantly recognise and can fill in with specific X and Y, depending on the context. *What's this fly doing in my soup* is the classic example but also *what's your sock doing on my desk, what's this student doing outside my office, what's that bus doing in this lane.* This is very simplistic but corpora of naturally occurring data tell us a lot about the formulaic and prefabricated ways in which we use language; ways that fly completely under the (human) radar, but which machines can extract rather well. Our brains sort of 'know' them, but our conscious minds do not.

It's without a doubt that machine translation has improved in leaps over the years. But does that mean human translators are no longer needed? No! First, machine translation systems still rely on the existence of massive amounts of training data needed by AI systems. In practice, that leads to varying quality in translation systems. Unsurprisingly, machine translation tools replicate existing language hierarchies, where some languages become the 'have-s' and others 'the-have-not-s' or 'the-have-less' (Seargeant, 2024, pp. 126–127).

Secondly, although machines can greatly speed up the translation process, it's humans with inside knowledge that can pick out the best choice. Humans are more than just probabilistic turn-handles, they really 'feel' the right way to translate something and can make good decisions on tricky, borderline examples.

This is important because there is more to translation than a match between form A in one language (**source language**) and form B in another language (**target language**). Translation is a two-pronged problem: (1) how to choose the best text to ensure fidelity to the original form and replicate its intended meaning and (2) how to choose the best text that sounds natural in the target language and carries the equivalent emotion and tone of the source language. Often a compromise needs to be reached between satisfying these two ideals. Humans remain the best agents to make those decisions, at least at the time of writing.

NATURAL LANGUAGE PROCESSING, CHATBOTS AND SOCIAL ROBOTS

Although machine translation appears to be one of the first language tasks for which machines have been enlisted, today, machines do so much more. We use computers to process natural language in various ways, from summarising and synthetising information to parsing and even producing new language in a conversational-like fashion.

As I'm sitting in a café to write parts of this chapter, I can overhear the barista 'speak' into his phone and command Siri to play some music. A few hours later, I will be sitting down for lunch, and a robot waiter will scoot over and 'serve' me my food as well as check that everything is in order with my meal. This is the world we currently live in; I wonder what the future will hold.

Looking back, we can already talk about generations of chatbots. Designed in the 1960s by MIT computer scientist Joseph Weizenbaum, ELIZA is hailed as the first chatbot. ELIZA was programmed to 'converse' in what looks remarkably like human speech. Here is an example from David Gunkel's book of how an interaction with this first chat bot might go (2025, p. 34):

Eliza: Hello, I am ELIZA.
User: Hello, Eliza.
Eliza: How are you today? What would you like to discuss?
User: I want to discuss chatbots.
Eliza: What would it mean to you if you got to discuss chatbots?
User: Maybe I would understand how they work.
Eliza: What is it you really want to know?
User: Are you a chatbot?
Eliza: Why are you interested in whether or not I am a chatbot?

It may feel like the exchange is going nowhere, but it must be said that it resembles many (human-to-human) conversations. To my mind, the only striking difference between this exchange and a regular spontaneous conversation is the presence of complete sentences, which we would not normally find in unplanned (human-to-human) conversations.

ELIZA was just the start, the gateway that gave us many other chatbots to come, from Amazon's Alexa, Google Assistant to Microsoft's Cortana, Samsung's Bixby and Apple's Siri. Some chatbots are programmed to produce only text, others can 'speak'. They might even 'speak' in your favourite accent if your preference includes the dialects associated with higher prestige and deeper pockets, deep enough to afford building their own technological resources. Other chatbots have physical bodies that can move around a room simulating actual people. My former professor, who is now the head of a prestigious German research institute has a physical robot walk around the halls and offices of his building while he is away. His robotic-self travels around holding an iPad with a video-chat window open that allows him to 'speak' with people simulating his physical presence even when he is absent. It impresses and freaks them out in equal measure.

The terms *chatbot*, *virtual assistant* and *social robot* roughly refer to the same thing, but their precise definition and associations differ depending on the context. Some people reserve the term 'robot' for a machine with a physical body. 'Chatbots' are typically thought of as programs that automatically post content to social media, sometimes also understood to falsely appear as human users. Virtual assistants are programs designed to serve companies, saving them time and money. Their chatbots interact with potential customers, answering questions and making product suggestions.

Virtual reality is everywhere and some of its uses are wonderful, for example, helping people overcome anxiety, loneliness or simply providing information quickly, round the clock. Others are creepy; think surveillance and other theft of personal or public information. And some can lead to uncomfortable dinner conversations, like the RealDoll sex robot.

As technologies will only improve and permeate all aspects of our lives, various social and ethical questions arise. First is the question of racial and linguistic discrimination: many of the chatbots resemble and perpetuate stereotypes associated with females (the ever helpful, polite and sexy secretary) while also increasing the status and power of hegemonic racial dominance (current chatbots have been noted to 'sound' white, see Chapter 5).

Secondly, there is the issue of accountability and morality. Is it ok to abuse a chatbot in various ways? What happens when a chatbot commits a crime of sorts, who should be held responsible and how?

LLMs, AI, DEATH OF THE AUTHOR AND THE RISE OF PROMPT ENGINEERS

By far the most significant technological development in this area has to do with the use of **Large Language Models** (LLMs). Although most people may have heard the term, few probably understand what they really are or how they work. My intention here is not to explain how LLMs work – David Gunkel's book has an excellent introductory chapter on this – but rather to spell out several issues arising specifically for language and language research from the use of these more sophisticated models.

As mentioned earlier, the incremental improvement in how technology and algorithms handle language data has meant that it's now impossible to reliably identify whether a given text was produced by human or machine.

For those of us grading assignments and essays, running submitted student work through a software like Turnitin could tell us – with evidence – where certain parts might have been copied and reproduced from. But LLMs operate in such a way that they can remix and recombine language phrases without being able to have these matched to original sources. As I write this, universities are trying out software which supposedly can provide a percentage of certainty that a given part of an assignment may have been produced by AI but really, most of us are extremely sceptical of this endeavour.

Increasingly, this type of machine help is becoming commonplace whereby AI tools are acting as editing assistants, not unlike spell-checking tools. Will there be a day when we will berate our students for not using AI to fix their writing in the way we scorn them when they have clearly not used spell-checkers?

The question then becomes this. Is it really their writing at that point? If a text is written by a person initially and subsequently edited with the help of suggestions from AI that is one thing, but if the process is the other way around, AI is asked to produce the first draft, which is then edited by a human, that seems like a different exercise entirely. Already, we see research articles that list ChatGPT as a co-author and academic journals encourage disclosing when AI tools are used to write parts (or all) of the text.

The idea that authorship is dead is by no means a new and looming threat. By some accounts, this was a done deal years ago. In fact, more than 50 years ago, in 1967 to be precise, in an essay by Roland Barthes, entitled *Death of the author*. Well before the existence of LLMs, Barthes begun deconstructing the primary role of authors as meaning-making agents. "The birth of the reader must be at the cost of the death of the Author", he wrote (1967, p. 148). According to him and many that followed, meaning doesn't just reside with the author, but it also arises from the reader and the context in which the text is interpreted. In the 1980s, Derrida extended these ideas to call attention to the ever-moving, ephemeral meaning of a text.

Take any novel by Jane Austen or Charles Dickens, Lev Tolstoi, Jean-Pierre Camus and many others and consider the shifting interpretations and reinterpretations that we have assigned to these books over the years. Seen with modern eyes, these stories take on new meanings and a life of their own. Meaning is socially constructed, emergent and evolving.

One might argue that LLMs have just put into practice what people like Barthes and Derrida have been arguing on paper all along. In a 2025 article, David Gunkel explains that LLMs do not generate language *de novo* but instead, remix and recycle existing texts to produce new combinations and recombinations of what has been said and written before. He argues that the figure of the "solitary author" is nothing but "a modern conceit" and that even though "the emergence of algorithmic co-creation may feel disorienting, [...] it is not entirely without precedent" (2025b, pp. 32–34). And writing is just one creative domain where this is taking place, according to Gunkel, these processes 'have shaped art, artistry, and authorship for centuries'. This has me wondering if I should have asked ChatGPT to write this very chapter for me. According to people like Gunkel, all future writing will become a collaborative enterprise between human and machine.

It's easy to see why this is happening too. The desire for speed in production can rapidly leave us thinking that we no longer have time to write full documents and we no longer have time to read full-length books. Just now, as I opened the PDF file containing Gunkel's article, I was faced with an automatically generated suggestion: "This appears to be a long document. Save time by reading a summary using AI Assistant". No thanks, I thought to myself. Will life speed up so much that my answer will eventually change to "yes, please"? Will the future bring the "Death of the Reader" too? Will the birth of AI come at the cost of both the author and the reader? Has that happened already?

Perhaps what we are seeing is not a death but a rebirth in a different role. It could be that the role of authors is changing from creators of content to creators of prompts. One consequence of the popularity of LLMs is the realisation that much of the output generated relies on the initial question fed into the machine. As the computing mantra goes 'garbage in, garbage out'. As many are realising from their experience with AI tools, different prompts lead to different outputs and crafting prompts is itself a language problem: the wording matters! It seems increasingly common to come across terms like 'prompt engineer'. Is this a new imagination for what we once called 'writer'?

LANGUAGE IN THE FUTURE

As we spend more time interacting via screens, collaborating with chatbots and using AI tools, there is increasing awareness that the language is changing to reflect our changing modern life.

It's no secret that our (increasingly online) dictionaries are being flooded with many terms that have either started out life online or relate to events and activities involving machines or the virtual world. For example, the latest words being added this year (2025) in the *Cambridge Dictionary* include *skibidi* ('a nonsense, playful phrase'), *delulu* ('delusional') and *tradwife* ('stay at home wife who makes extra income by posting online content'); all of which have online connections. Last year, *Duden*, the most well-respected dictionary of standard German added words like *ChatGPT*, *Hyperloop*, *Triggerwarnung* ('trigger warning') and *ghosting* (in addition to words related to cooking, war and crisis). Earlier this year, the French dictionary *Le Petit Robert* added words like *démission silencieuse* (originating on TikTok, a translation of the phrase 'quiet quitting' referring to employees who invest as little loyalty and time as possible into their work), *débunker* ('debunk'), *neobanque* ('digital bank'), *hypertrucage* ('deepfake'), as well as AI terms like *hallucination* ('a false answer produced by AI') and *prompter* ('the action of generating a prompt').

And there's more. It's not just that we need new words to talk about our increasingly interlinked machine-human world, but ironically, we also need to invent new words to evade the very algorithms that we created. As Adam Aleksic explains in his book and TEDx talk, because algorithms are used on social media to flag taboo, sensitive or censored topics, users are working hard to invent new words and outsmart them.

Aleksic's opening example is the word *unalive*, meaning 'to kill'. According to him, its first use dates to 2013, in an episode of *Ultimate Spider-Man*, which then saw it being taken up in an online meme that eventually went viral on social media in 2021, following TikTok's stringent rules on taboo words and sensitive topics, especially posts talking about suicide. Of course, euphemisms for death or dying are not a new thing. English and plenty of other languages have a myriad of ways in which speakers can avoid explicitly uttering the word *death*, often indirect and idiomatic phrases like *kick the bucket*, *pass away*, *sleep with the fishes, lose the battle, buy the farm, be in a better place* and so on. What is different about *unalive* is that it was created specifically to outwit the algorithms. This is language change driven by machines, and ironically, also spread all over the globe with their help.

Because algorithms can block content that violates the rules of social media platforms, users adapt to avoid detection, and they need to do so constantly as algorithms change fast. From unconventional spellings like *p3nis* and *pen1s* to emoji 🍆 and brand-new words, users are relentlessly evolving the language they use to ensure they can still express what they want. Many of the newly minted innovations make it out of the virtual world into everyday conversations and even other forms of writing, much to the surprise and sometimes despair of some speakers.

Added to that, algorithms are also heavily involved in promoting content, a factor which is itself a driver of change. Influencers, for instance tradwives (stay at home mums who make money from posting online content) are sensitive to which of their content does well in engaging wide attention. They are also aware of the power of innovation.

Innovation is linked to increased attention as we need constant doses of 'new'. Little dopamine hits feed the obsession with scrolling and clicking. Even the smallest innovation can grab our attention because we are primed to associate a given word or turn of phrase with interesting trends. Phrases like *no because* constitute a classic example. Rumoured to have started out on TikTok, this new turn of phrase is a **discourse marker** (a word or phrase used to organise the discourse and sometimes buy thinking time, like *I mean* or *you know*), that has become the hallmark of media-savvy influencers. It's not taken long for this phrase to be used in IRL ('in real life'), which is to say in face-to-face conversations. Even hashtags, which were deliberately devised in 2004 as hyperlinks connecting similar posts and like-minded groups are now used in everyday conversations and other genres. #yestheyare #andwhynot.

It's impossible to predict what the language of the future will look like. This difficulty is not new. The outcome of language change has never been predictable. The factors that are driving language change today are perhaps closer to science fiction stories than were once deemed possible.

Yet the ongoing relationship between language and technology is also not new. Writing was the first major technology to transform language, and people were certainly not happy about it. Socrates thought committing language to paper would "ruin people's memories and weaken their minds" (Seargeant, 2024, p. 16). Every new technology is disruptive, causing changes of various kinds, including changes in how we communicate. But ultimately, language is a human enterprise and while machines may be able to mimic this ability and even influence the way it changes, the heart and consciousness of language remain a human endeavour.

WANT MORE?

- Read David Gunkel's 2025 book *AI for Communication* and Philip Seargeant's 2024 book *The Future of Language.*
- Watch Adam Aleksic's Ted Ed Lesson "Are we cooked? How social media shapes your language" (https://www.ted.com/talks/adam_aleksic_are_we_cooked_how_social_media_shapes_your_language).
- Listen to Emily Bender unpacking NLP and its ethics on Episode 16 of the Radical AI podcast (https://www.radicalai.org/e16-emily-bender).

9

LANGUAGE ATTITUDES

Do you think the wife of former Australian Prime Minister Malcolm Turnbull is *delicious*? Apparently, former French President Macron does. Or maybe he doesn't, the point is that he said he did. This slip of tongue happened during a press conference while he was visiting Australia in 2018. Apparently, what he meant to say was that she was *delightful* but made a mistake switching between French *délicieuse* and English *delightful*. *Délicieuse* can mean both *delightful* and *delicious*; it's all about context. This partial semantic overlap between *délicieuse* and *delicious* (Chapter 7) will be immediately obvious to any French/English bilingual, but will the world let Macron forget his mistake? Not a chance!

When it comes to language, many of us can easily become harsh and opinionated critics. We use language as a yardstick for evaluating others, from how smart or trustworthy they sound, to how friendly, funny or even suitable as a mate they might be. People have strong feelings about language and make snap judgements about how everyone else is using it. We even make judgements about the languages themselves: *Italian is so sexy, Russian is so harsh.* In this final chapter, I hope to convince you that everything about language is imbued with attitudes and beliefs, some accurate, some not so accurate, but none completely neutral.

LANGUAGE IS A SOCIAL CUE, JUST ASK (YOUR) CHILDREN

From a very young age, we prefer to hear not only a familiar voice but also a familiar language, dialect and even accent. Newborns

DOI: 10.4324/9781003621485-9

orient themselves towards their mother's voice and towards speech in the language(s) they are learning (see Chapter 7). By six months old, they even show preferences towards their own dialect over a mutually intelligible but distinct one, for example, preferring Australian English over South African English or American English (DeJesus et al., 2022, p. 237).

Experiments tell us that young children begin to form various **language attitudes** and that they begin to use language to make inferences about others. They will use **accent**, a speaker's distinctive pronunciation, to infer their geographical location and go as far as using the strength of their accent to infer their relative distance from the child's own region. It's astounding that children can make such sophisticated inferences.

Uncovering these insights is not straightforward because it's not always possible or even sensible to ask children direct questions about language attitudes and beliefs. These difficulties arise for various reasons, but here are at least three. First, some of the questions are too abstract and difficult to understand. Second, some questions are culturally sensitive, and children will feel compelled to tell the researcher what they perceive to be the 'right answer'. And third, children – much like adults – don't consciously think about the beliefs they have in the first place, so retrieving them and putting them into words can be difficult.

Scholars have devised weird and wonderful ways to get around these issues in order to probe attitudes. For example, in a series of studies called the **switched-at-birth task**, Lawrence Hirschfeld and Susan Gelman (1997) presented children of varying ages with an imagined scenario where a child born to English-speaking parents was switched at birth, say at the hospital, with another, born to Portuguese-speaking parents. The question asked was which language would the child grow up to speak?

Typically, three-year-old children chose randomly between the two languages, but by five years of age, children consistently began to choose the language of the parents raising the child rather than that of the biological parents. Put simply, by five years, children already know that language is not a biological and immutable trait determined by genes, like the colour of your eyes or hair, but rather a cultural trait that can be radically influenced by the environment in which you are brought up.

At roughly the same time, children develop another interesting set of beliefs. Jasmine DeJesus, Katherine Kinzler and colleagues have shown (see review in DeJesus et al., 2022, chapter 15) that by five years, children reach the conclusion that some people 'sound nice' while some people 'sound smart'. But here's the rub: no group has both qualities; speakers are either judged to be nice (and not smart) or judged to be smart (and not so nice).

Incidentally, this nice/smart division persists into adulthood, and it is recurrently found in languages and cultures all over the world. In the United States, this perception splits the country geographically. Southerners are thought to be nice, warm and friendly, while Northerners are evaluated as smart, competent and (better) educated. In the UK, there is a nice/smart distinction between Cockney and Multicultural London English (see Chapter 6) on the one hand and **Received Pronunciation** (RP, sometimes also assumed to be the Queen's English) on the other. In China, northeastern Mandarin dialects contrast in this way with standard Chinese.

In general, it's not surprising that children orient themselves towards adult norms when it comes to language. After all, language acquisition starts with adults in the first place. It's also unsurprising that they prefer their **native language** (mother tongue) or accent over a foreign one, given that we are primed for familiarity. We trust people we know better, and a shared language is a cue for a shared social group.

What is surprising is the level of sophistication that even relatively young children display in their ability to identify and distinguish closely related dialects, even in cases when they can't yet name the dialects in question. They may not be able to articulate language attitudes in refined ways, but they sure can make highly nuanced inferences.

The orientation towards adult norms continues as children start school and teachers champion the higher prestige variety of the language, typically the standard version. It is this standard that young pupils are taught as they learn to read and write. They are also taught that it's this standard that is the 'correct', 'proper' or 'better' version of the language. The idea is subtle but not trivial; literacy doesn't just facilitate the ability to read and write but also an overt sense of evaluation and judgement of language forms.

Between the ages of eight and 12 years, children begin to hold multiple and sometimes conflicting ideas about language. On the one hand, they continue to acquire the 'correct' and 'proper' (**overt prestige**) forms from teachers and other adults. On the other hand, a new influence appears on their radar: the peer group. This group typically uses distinctive forms, sometimes taboo words, expletives and swear words, non-standard or regional pronunciations and maybe different grammar too. This kind of language constitutes localised ways of speaking (Chapter 5) and 'cool speak', demarcating its users as central members of the group, whose attention and friendship are desirable and valued (**covert prestige**).

Although the overall picture is typically more complex and variable than this simple sketch suggests, it's easy to see how early diverging influences between adult norms and peer group, as well as differences between formal contexts and informal interactions give rise to a nice/smart as well as us/them division in evaluating language use. Beginning as early as childhood, we learn to treat language as a social cue for evaluating others. And once started, we never stop.

FEELINGS ABOUT LANGUAGES, FEELINGS ABOUT SPEAKERS

It was back in the 1930s that researchers started to test what judgements people make about others based on their voices alone (Dragojevic et al., 2021). Such judgements involved using someone's voice to gauge social attributes, like the speaker's gender, class, age or ethnicity. And people usually get this information right.

The second finding was that they also make judgements about a speaker's personality and character based on their voice. But this time, they get it wildly wrong. Interestingly, although the judgements made are typically incorrect, they are wrong in the same direction, being extremely consistent with each other. For instance, people might all agree that a particular accent is uneducated or lazy and judge the speaker using it to be uneducated or lazy, yet this would then turn out to be completely inaccurate. This early work suggested that language attitudes are rooted in stereotypes and not representative of (authentic) personality traits. The disappointment that followed left language attitude research all but abandoned.

Fast forward 30 years, and come the 1960s, a new technique reignited fresh interest in the field. In order to fully appreciate its potential, let's consider two important problems in eliciting language attitudes. First problem, participants are likely to tell you what they believe you want to hear or what is perceived as the 'right answer'. Second problem, when eliciting evaluations of a speaker, it is difficult to disentangle how participants feel about the speaker's social traits, (say) gender or ethnicity, from how they feel about their language use. All these identities are bundled into single individuals (Chapter 5) and one voice, so it's hard to tease them apart.

Now enter the **Matched-Guise technique**. Devised by Wallace Lambert and his colleagues (Lambert et al., 1960), this method built on existing methods in a cunning way. With Matched-Guise techniques, rather than using distinct **guises** (voices) produced by different speakers (who may differ from each other not just in their accent or language, but also their age, gender or ethnicity), unbeknownst to participants, the guises heard were produced by one and the same speaker; chosen for their ability to perform different accents or multiple languages. The guises are in this sense 'matched' to the same speaker, which allows the researcher to control everything else about the speaker, their gender, age, class, ethnicity and so on and thus allowing evaluations of the actual language use (alone) to emerge, without influence from other traits.

Specifically, Lambert was interested to know what English- and French-Canadian speakers thought about French and English speakers. It would be pointless to just walk up to a random Canadian and ask them such a question directly because the issue is both politically sensitive and too abstract to answer off the cuff. However, a Matched-Guise technique allows for more accurate evaluations of the languages to surface because participants can rate specific voices in a controlled manner, disentangled from other speaker attributes.

Lambrecht and his team found that both English- and French-Canadians prefer English guises over French ones, which is surprising because one might have expected French-Canadians to prefer their own language over English. Participants were asked to rate the guises (which were performed by the same speaker, a bilingual proficient in both Canadian French and Canadian English) on 14 different characteristics, ranging from leadership, ambition, dependability and confidence to height, good looks, sense of humour, entertainability and kindness. English came up on top for most characteristics across both groups of speakers. What is more, the

French speakers rated the French guise even lower than the English speakers had rated it. I cannot help but wonder if Canadians may have revised their attitudes since the 1960s.

We can ask all sorts of questions about these findings, but the million-dollar question is why French speakers feel this way about their own language. The answer is not straightforward, and we can of course only speculate about it, but it is by no means unusual either. Such **linguistic insecurity** can be found all over the world. For example, in Aotearoa New Zealand, the local variety of English spoken, called New Zealand English, used to be seen as less prestigious and less educated (the 'dreadful colonial twang' was one common reference to it) compared to RP. Similarly, Singapore Colloquial English or Singlish, the local Singaporean dialect of English, which blends English with features of Chinese and Malay, also received negative press initially and still does, depending on who you ask, scoring low on the 'smart' scale compared to RP.

In time, these local varieties have become more accepted, and the social desirability of sounding local has ameliorated somewhat, but not completely, the linguistic insecurity that speakers feel about their own dialect. By way of illustration, in April 2019, an online tourism company deemed New Zealand English the sexiest accent in the world. Apparently, no one was more shocked by this finding than New Zealanders themselves. The local media had a field day with the announcement, replaying scenes from famous romantic movies dubbed with New Zealand accents and mocking the supposed ridiculousness of the idea. Hiding beneath the humour was a bashful country collectively taking a breath at the thought that an accent once tarnished by 'cultural cringe' could ever be sported as a sex symbol.

Another source of linguistic insecurity arises from attitudes towards profanity and expletives, the perennial 'bad language'. But can language ever really be 'bad'? One recent study looked at the use of such language online and compared various dialects of English. The top English swearing nations are not that important (but if you really must know the United States comes up first, followed by Great Britain and Australia for overall amount of profanity). What's interesting is that there are cultural differences even among English speakers. Martin Schweinberger and Kate Burridge (2025a) found no fewer than 597 different swear words. Swearing is not just about being creative, but it is also a natural and normal part of how we use language. Yes, swearing can of course be very offensive in some contexts, but it also serves useful functions, such as building rapport and fostering closeness, entertainment and humour, easing tension and mitigating pain. As is often the case with language, it all depends on audience and context. Nevertheless, that does not stop some people from judging others for their swearing behaviour.

On the other hand, not all language attitudes lead to **linguistic insecurity**. For example, a language study in Saudi Arabia by Laila Alhazmi (2023) revealed that speakers of the Najdi dialect rate their own dialect as being easier to understand than other dialects of Arabic, the least harsh-sounding and the least uncultured. In other words, they rated their own speech very highly. But on what scale; is this 'nice' or is it 'smart'? It's difficult to know exactly on which of these axes Najdi sits because intelligibility, harshness and being cultured do not fall neatly in either the 'nice' (sometimes called **solidarity**) or the 'smart' (or **prestige**) dimension. Regardless, the point stands that some speakers are indeed positive and confident about their own dialect, while others are not.

Linguistic confidence: while some speakers coyly resist it, others try to engineer it. In 2017, the BBC launched a new station in its Nigerian branch, broadcasting in West African Pidgin English (WAPE). WAPE has little traction in the official sense of the word because no country designates it as an official language (more on this later), but despite this, it functions as a **lingua franca** throughout West Africa, allowing speakers to communicate with one another when they do not share a common language.

WAPE is a Pidgin (Chapter 6) based on English, combining English words with structural features from various local African languages, including Nigerian, Ghanaian, Cameroonian and others. WAPE is not one single language but several; it is in fact a group of related Pidgins, which are mutually intelligible but nevertheless distinct, being based on different local languages.

So, when the BBC adjusted its broadcasting language to include WAPE, how did they do it, and how do speakers of WAPE feel about this move? Folajimi Oyebola and Kingsley Ugwuanyi (2023) set out to investigate precisely these questions by means of questionnaires, distributed to university students. Their findings suggest that speakers of WAPE were generally positive about a BBC Pidgin channel, welcoming the increased prestige and legitimising of WAPE that came with being used by a renowned corporation.

However, they also had reservations, one being that the version used by the BBC was closer to Nigerian Pidgin and not representative of other Pidgins, which broadly make up the WAPE space. Some of the participants viewed BBC Pidgin as "a standardised and upgraded version, mostly used by the elites who want to also communicate in pidgin", viewing it as "closer to Standard English" (Oyebola & Ugwuanyi, 2023, p. 94). Others thought BBC Pidgin was 'good but not as sweet as normal N[igerian] P[idgin]'. The words 'upgraded' and 'sweet' are significant. These words describe how speakers feel about it, rather than telling us something objective about the linguistic characteristics of the language.

And these quotes subtly point to a potential price that comes with increased prestige: a move towards a more standard version of a colloquial lingua franca, and towards a version of the language that backgrounds the varied identities of its speakers. Speakers worried that what was once an informal code connecting common, everyday people may become a symbol of power in the hands of the elites. These observations highlight ways in which language attitudes can drive and shape language change and influence the status and function of a language.

It is fair to say that since the 1960s, research probing language attitudes has ramped up. Alongside questionnaires and Matched-Guise techniques, other methods are utilised nowadays, from surveys to map-drawing tasks (see next section) and other gamified approaches whose purpose is to allow evaluations to emerge even when speakers are wary to provide them directly.

In that time, the field has expanded to consider three main types of attitudes that speakers hold in relation to language use: attitudes about speakers of a particular language (*speakers of Latin are so cultured, Italians sound so sexy*), attitudes about the languages themselves (*Mandarin is one of the hardest languages to learn, BBC Pidgin is not as sweet*) and attitudes about changes that are taking place within a language (*Turkish is being diluted by too many words borrowed from English*) (see Figure 9.1). Most research seems to have centred on beliefs about speakers of certain languages or varieties, but as might be expected, all three types are interconnected.

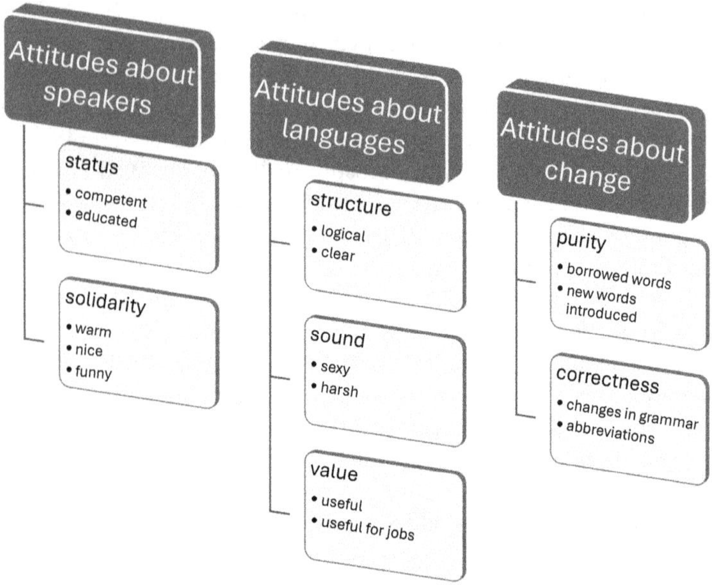

Figure 9.1 Various attitudes held in relation to language use

FOLK BELIEFS ABOUT LANGUAGE

A related notion concerns beliefs that people hold with respect to the number of dialects of a given language and the regions where these dialects are spoken. Take, for instance, the island of Cyprus. One of the most widely spoken languages in Cyprus is Greek. But is it the same language as that spoken in Greece, and is it just one single language or several distinct languages? You could ask a linguist to give you a linguistic classification, but what do the inhabitants of the island think?

The 'folk', as lay people are sometimes labelled, have their own opinions about what it is that people in their country or region speak. These beliefs matter because they can influence government policy and legislation, planning efforts and documentation projects, among other things.

As far as Cyprus is concerned, Modern Greek is an **official language** of the country, alongside Turkish. This means that Modern Greek is officially designated by the country's government as an important language for the island nation. You can think of this as the language spoken in today's Greece, but with a Cypriot accent. Alongside this official version, we also hear another variety of Greek: Cypriot Greek. While Modern Greek is the language of formal interactions, used in schools, government business, media, newspapers and television, Cypriot Greek is used in informal ones, in the street and marketplaces and in people's homes. It is also what young infants learn as a mother tongue, before they attend school (where they learn Modern Greek).

Yet the two languages are sufficiently distinct to have different labels and to lack mutual intelligibility. Cypriots are raised with both languages, and knowledge of Modern Greek has increased, especially since primary schooling became compulsory in 1962. The situation in which a country's population navigates two codes is called **diglossia**, itself a Greek word originally, derived from *di-* meaning two and *glôssa* meaning language or tongue. Other examples of diglossic nations include Arabic-speaking countries like Egypt, Morocco and the United Arab Emirates and countries like Bangladesh and Malaysia.

Constantina Fotiou and Kleanthes Grohmann (2022) conducted in-depth interviews with Greek speakers in their town of Nicosia to probe perceptions of language use throughout Cyprus. Among other things, they wanted to know how many Greek dialect regions would be identified by Nicosia residents throughout the island, what characteristics they associated with each one, and which dialect was deemed to be most socially acceptable and prestigious.

They interviewed 30 participants, asking them directly about their thoughts, but also included an additional task: the **draw-a-map-task**, first introduced by Dennis Preston in the 1980s (Preston, 1981). This task involved providing participants with a blank map of Cyprus and asking them to draw regions dividing the country by dialect.

The participants interviewed produced no fewer than 25 distinct regions dividing up their island (an area of roughly 9,251 km^2). Clearly, Nicosia residents were operating with different beliefs about which languages are spoken in Cyprus than linguists. More than that, they varied from each other in their beliefs too. Some participants refused to draw any regional dialect boundaries at all, because they felt there were no real separate dialects spoken. Any one person drew on average about four regions, but overall, the regions were drawn in different parts of the map with little agreement.

Another finding that emerged from the interviews was that alongside Modern Greek as the **high variety** (the more prestigious form, also called Standard Cypriot Greek), further distinctions were made along a continuum between a **low variety** of Cypriot Greek which was seen as the 'tidied-up' and 'polite' lingua franca, and another dialect, described as 'peasantry' or 'heavy' Cypriot Greek (a code that contained more regional features, depending on where on the island it was spoken).

Which dialect was rated the most prestigious and socially acceptable? The local Nicosia dialect. Given that the participants interviewed were themselves from that region, this meant that participants rated their own variety highest. Unlike the linguistic insecurity scenarios discussed earlier, there are good reasons why someone may rate their own accent highly. First, people typically hear their accent most often and thus perceive it as being the most neutral, the default. In fact, many people feel (and say) that they have no accent at all. Don't believe it; it's a myth, not reality. Everyone has an accent, whether they perceive it or not.

Another reason why the Nicosia dialect was rated so highly could be because it is centrally located, and overall, central dialects of Cyprus were rated as more prestigious compared to rural or more geographically peripheral ones, for example, compared to the dialect spoken in Ammochostos.

The rural versus urban distinction is a very interesting one when it comes to language attitudes. As a rule of thumb, rural communities are often perceived as an imagined idyll, whereby language is struck in its purest form, preserving traditional usage and unspoiled by the assumed urban corruptions that infect large cities. Of course, this is just the idealised version of the rural landscape, and in many places, it is completely different from reality.

While urban centres are associated with dynamic change and modernity (Chapter 6), sometimes also with wealth and the elites, rural communities – and by association, their speech – are associated with pejorative stereotypes stemming from isolation, being backward and conservative. For example, people living in rural United States are sometimes disparagingly labelled as 'hick', 'hillbilly' or 'redneck' (a term also applied to certain Australian rural people, especially those deemed to be unworldly, unsophisticated and overwhelmingly white). In Trinidad, rural communities may be derogatorily referred to as 'bush' or 'coolie'. Labels like this can be found all over the world. The rural versus urban divide is an example of 'us versus them', and this extends to speech styles also.

Naturally, these are just stereotypes and not objective. Take the isolation aspect. Not all rural communities are isolated, and in fact, some have regular and varying levels of contact with neighbouring communities. Contact may arise from consumption of mass media, travel between localities due to work or education opportunities and intermarriage.

Contact often (though not always) leads to changes in the language that mirror other social changes in the fabric of the community. For example, in rural Scotland, regional Doric dialect features are being lost to standard Scottish ones due to increased influence from urban centres (Gordon, 2019, p. 444). In Canada, Newfoundland rural English forms are also shifting towards more standard Canadian English patterns (Gordon, 2019, p. 446).

But not all contact leads to change or loss. Take the Sui people in China. As Matthew Gordon's (2019) review article explains, the Sui people live in a culture where women move for marriage to their husband's village, a practice called exogamy. For those that go on to have children, mothers typically keep speaking their Sui dialect, while children acquire the dialect of Sui that their fathers and local community use. The two dialects are mutually intelligible, and this facilitates the maintenance of variation. However, speakers of Zhuang, another exogamous people, do the opposite, whereby when mothers move, they change their dialect to match their husbands and local village dialect (possibly because, unlike Sui, their dialects are not mutually intelligible). So even within the same language family, and rural areas, we find variation arising in situations of contact between different communities.

The rural/urban divide seems to be relevant in Aotearoa New Zealand also. One study using the draw-a-map task, conducted a decade ago, has shown that speakers mapped dialects alongside rural/urban and social class distinctions. Marie-France Duhamel and Miriam Meyerhoff (2015) analysed regional dialect maps collected by university students through their social networks, identifying dialects of New Zealand English and found many more dialects than linguists had previously posited. How can that be?

As far as linguists are concerned (Bauer & Bauer, 2002), Aotearoa New Zealand can be divided into three different dialect regions: a Northern dialect, a central dialect and a Southern dialect. However, the 'folk' divided it into seven regions (though not everyone identified all seven, most people divided the map into four areas): Northland, Auckland, Waikato/Hamilton, Eastern North Island, Wellington, Christchurch, Southland & Otago/South Island. The main distinction seemed to be between vast rural areas (Northland, Waikato, Eastern North Island, Southland & Otago) and big urban centres (Auckland, Hamilton, Wellington and Christchurch). Clearly, while linguists are thinking about language features, the folk are thinking about social groupings.

As far as attitudes were concerned, the rural dialects were seen as the "more pronounced accent", the "farmer accent", or "typical New Zealand accent", while the urban ones were the default, "neutral choice", "fast" and "business like" speech (Duhamel & Meyerhoff, 2015, p. 241).

The main point here is not about who is right (scholars or the folk), but rather what speaker perceptions tell us about New Zealand society more generally. Traditionally, New Zealanders like to project an egalitarian society, where social classes exhibit little separation, presenting an even playing field of equal opportunities for all citizens. However, exploring attitudes towards dialect variation helps to illuminate a picture of an increasingly divergent society, growing inequality and an emerging ideology concerned with the existence of social classes.

INSTITUTIONAL BELIEFS ABOUT LANGUAGE

A completely different set of values and attitudes concerns ideology regarding the process of borrowing. When speakers of two languages come into regular contact with one another, it is common to observe transfer of features between the languages in question. Such transfer can involve any linguistic material, from words (lexis) to phrases, borrowing words like *café* (from French), *sushi* (from Japanese) and *Safari* (from Swahili), phrases like *Carpe Diem* (from Latin) and *Hasta la vista* (from Spanish) and even grammar (like adding suffixes for marking plural forms on Domari and Romani nouns, borrowed from Arabic, Matras, 2009, pp. 8–9).

The most common one and the most salient for speakers themselves is the first in that list, namely, lexical borrowing or **loanwords**. It does not take a linguist to note that English adopts words from other languages, for instance *croissant* and *government* from French, *zero* and *sugar* from Arabic, *lager* and *hamburger* from German, *pepper* and *banyan* from Sanskrit. In this sense, English is a **recipient language**, receiving loanwords. But English is also a **source language**, providing words to other languages: *iPad, computer, weekend* and *baby* are frequently borrowed into other languages, like French, German and Spanish (for more examples, see the *World Online Loanword Database*, Haspelmath & Tadmor, 2009).

Not everyone is thrilled about loanwords because they can be seen as encroaching on existing vocabulary and diluting the purity of the language they are entering. The *Académie Française* 'French Academy' is most famously noted (and often ridiculed) for its strict ban on foreign words entering French, especially words coming from English, also known as **anglicisms**. But purist French speakers are not the only ones concerned about incoming anglicisms; other language academies and other prescriptive bodies share such concerns, as do speakers of German, Turkish, Italian, Japanese and Welsh.

Ironically, there is equal concern about English being weakened and deteriorated by loanwords from other languages. And this concern is by no means a recent one. David Crystal wrote in a 2006 book about a fourteenth-century Benedictine Monk, Ranulph Hidgen, who proclaimed that mixing with the Danes and, in due course, with the Normans would lead to the erosion of English. Fast forward to modern times and being a global lingua franca has its own pluses and minuses. Many English words are indeed being borrowed into other languages, but equally, English is learnt as a second language by millions of speakers of other languages, generating fresh fears that the language is being diluted by foreign elements.

Anxieties about language purity are reminiscent of ideology connected to nationhood and political affiliation. The idea that language is both a unifying force and a dividing one rings particularly true if we consider the ways that various dominant social groups assert their right to use a particular language. Certain small, but not insignificant acts are present in our every day that reinforce nationalism and the power of the state.

Language is often firmly embedded in these, but not always explicitly recognised as being so. For example, singing the national anthem entails the use of the language that is seen as emblematic of a political territory. Road signage in a town or locality entails the presence of one language (if the sign is monolingual) or of several (for multilingual states), and the order in which the sign presents the various languages can itself signal linguistic and, by association, cultural hierarchies. Mundane national symbols and words printed on local produce and on supermarket items constitute routine reminders of national identity by means of a kind of benign nationalism called **banal nationalism** by Michael Billig (1995).

Alongside the small acts of banal nationalism, nations and governments engage in much bigger acts too: language policies and language planning. Why do states have such policies, and how do these arise in the first place?

HOW "HEALTHY" IS YOUR LANGUAGE?

Languages are not animate beings with a body and soul. Yet they are sometimes characterised as though they were. Such anthropomorphic views lead scholars and language commissions to talk about languages needing protection, ensuring their survival and making provisions for their vitality. This is particularly true for languages in danger of becoming extinct.

Of the approximately 7,000 languages currently spoken around the globe, just under half are currently endangered, according to the *Ethnologue* (2025). But how do we know when a language is in danger?

Language death happens when the last speaker of a given language dies, taking the language with them. It's tempting to assume that the livelihood of a language depends on the number of its speakers. The more speakers there are, the "healthier" the language. To some extent this is true, but it's both more nuanced than this and more complicated.

Counting the total number of speakers is not all that meaningful on its own because not every speaker plays the same role in the language equation. If a language has mostly older speakers and they are not passing it on to the next generation, then the language is likely to die out along with the older generation. However, if the speakers are more evenly distributed across generations, in other words, if there is **inter-generational transmission**, then the language is likely to keep being passed on to children, who then pass it on to their children and so on. This is what a thriving language picture looks like. In addition, it also depends on whether speakers are likely to marry within the same linguistic community or not, which will, in turn, influence transmission. Rates and sources of migration also matter.

Measuring the "health" of a language comes under the label of **linguistic vitality**. Estimates of linguistic vitality rely on more than just demographic factors and raw numbers of speakers. Two additional pillars of linguistic vitality are status and institutional support.

The status of a language is heavily enmeshed with attitudes relating to power, prestige and authority. Languages acquire status from their speakers. When speakers of a given language are associated with economic dominance and high social standing, then their language is seen as having high status too. The converse is also true. It is no coincidence that, for example, standard British English is largely based on the English spoken in and around London, where the British Parliament and seat of power are located.

There is also the pillar loosely termed institutional support. This refers to the resources that a state invests in supporting the language. For example, in Wales, the state-funded school immersion programme has been highly influential in boosting the numbers of Welsh speakers throughout the country. Following this strategy, on the other side of the world, the Māori Language Commission worked with the New Zealand government of the 1970s to form the *Kohanga Reo* 'language nests' immersion programmes to increase the number of Māori speakers in the country. Institutional support need not necessarily involve government bodies; it can also relate to informal organisations like cultural or religious groups, such as Hula dancing groups in Hawaii, Nahuatl religious practices in South America, or Breton-speaking Catholic groups in rural France (Davis, 2014).

Unsurprisingly, the three pillars are interconnected. When languages have high prestige, they are also likely to have higher rates of inter-generational transmission, higher numbers of speakers, more institutional support and generally attract positive attitudes. Conversely, when linguistic vitality is low, languages become at risk of endangerment. Reversing the trend and attempting to increase linguistic vitality (**language revitalisation**) involves planning efforts across all these same pillars.

One important dimension in language revitalisation relates to the legal provisions that nations make for the various languages spoken within their territory. There are many different legal designations that a state can adopt, but perhaps the most common one is specifying **official languages**, the languages used in government, education, media and other important formal business. Incidentally, the *Ethnologue* lists more than 12 different types of language provisions that nations can make.

Here are some examples. South Africa has 12 official languages: Afrikaans, English, isiNdebele, isiXhosa, isiZulu, Sepedi, Sesotho, Setswana, siSwati, Tshivenda, Xitsonga and South African Sign Language (SASL). The Pacific nation of Vanuatu has three official languages: Bislama (an English-based Creole, Chapter 6), English and French. Australia has no official language. How can that be? It's not because Australians have no language at all, but because English is the **de facto language**, it is the everyday language (a bit like an unwritten official language); but being so dominant, it needs no special status in law. As far as Aboriginal (Indigenous) languages are concerned, Australia has hundreds of these, many of them endangered, but having so many makes it difficult to specify all of them in law and ensure fairness for all speakers. In Aotearoa New Zealand, there are two official languages, Māori and New Zealand Sign Language (NZSL), and here also, English is a de facto language.

Conversely, while the law can improve the status of a language or dialect, it can also do the opposite and, albeit unwittingly, threaten the status of minority languages or non-standard dialects. For example, in the United States, the law makes it possible to discriminate based on accent, say in employment cases where an accent may stop candidates from successfully carrying out the job (Seargeant, 2024, p. 119). The hegemony of the standard dialect (accent) is further demonstrated by the existence of companies like Sanas, who offer AI solutions to apparently "translate your accent in real time" from a non-standard accent into a standard one (ibid). According to Sanas' website, "Accents make us who we are, but in certain situations can be challenging". The word "challenging" is clearly loaded here. But why would anyone want to "translate" their accent? Reading on, words like "clarity" and "intelligibility" come up, implying that non-standard accents are less clear and less easy to understand. By whom exactly? All these questions betray perceptions and attitudes that we hold in relation to language use and to what is evaluated as "better" or "clear" language.

Language is so much more than a mere transfer of information from one brain to another. We feel and exist through our languages. They represent a huge part of our identity and a crucial ingredient of who we are. Even the labels we attach to our languages matter.

It's no wonder that the feelings that speakers attach to their languages can be very strong, deep enough to write those languages into law, in a bid to garner support and recognition. The reality is that whether correct or incorrect, we all make judgements about others based on the language they use, and we hold various beliefs about what these languages might be like or should be like.

Whether we lose face through linguistic mishaps as French President Emmanuel Macron did in Australia, gain status by speaking dominant languages or plan and lobby to revitalise an endangered language fighting for survival, ultimately, language remains at the fabric of who we are as people, our identity, heritage and values.

WANT MORE?

- Read Nick Evans' book *Words of Wonder and What They Tell Us* (2022).
- Listen to the *Vocal Fries* podcast on linguistic discrimination hosted by Carrie Gillon and Megan Figueroa https://vocalfriespod.com/.
- Watch the documentary on Accent Bias produced by *The University of Edinburgh*: https://www.youtube.com/watch?v=vshZsrWearo.

REFERENCES

Adams, Douglas (1978). *The Hitch Hiker's guide to the galaxy*. Pan Books.

Aleksic, Adam (2025). *Algospeak: How social media is transforming the future of language*. Knopf.

Alhazmi, Laila Mobarak (2023). Language attitudes in fast-growing societies: New insights in the dynamism dimension. *Humanities and Social Sciences Communications 10*(1), 1–14. https://doi.org/10.1057/s41599-023-01988-1

Anderson, Stephen (2020). Do animals communicate using a language? In Laurie Bauer & Andreea S. Calude (Eds.) *Questions about language: What everyone should know about language in the 21st century* (pp. 4–17). Routledge.

Austin, John L. (1975). *How to do things with words*. Harvard University Press.

Baron, Naomi S. (2010). *Always on: Language in an online and mobile world*. Oxford University Press.

Barthes, Roland (1977). Death of the author. (originally published in 1976 and translated by S. Heath.). In S. Heath (Ed.) *Image, music, text* (pp. 142–148). Fontana.

Bauer, Laurie & Winifred Bauer (2002). The persistence of dialect areas. *Te Reo 45*, 37–44.

Bender, Emily & Hanna, Alex (2025). *The AI con: How to fight big tech's hype and create the future we want*. Random House.

Bender, Emily, Gebru, Timnit, McMillan-Major, Angelina & Shmitchell, Shmargaret (2021). On the dangers of stochastic parrots: Can language models be too big? 🦜. In *Proceedings of the 2021 ACM conference on fairness, accountability, and transparency* (pp. 610–623). https://doi.org/10.1145/3442188.3445922

Berko (Gleason), Jean (1958). The child's learning of English morphology. *Word 14*, 150–177.

Bernstein, Isaac (2024). Haitian Creole language courses coming to Princeton's French and Italian department in the next year. *The Daily Princetonian*. Accessed on 4 February 2026 from: https://www.dailyprincetonian.com/article/2024/11/princeton-news-stlife-haitian-creole-language-courses-french-department

Billig, Michael (1995). *Banal nationalism*. Sage.

Brook, Marisa & Blamire, Emily (2023). Language play is language variation: Quantitative evidence and what it implies about language change. *Language, 99*(3), 491–530. https://doi.org/10.1353/lan.2023.a907010

Brunetti, Lisa, Bott Stefan, Marcus, Costa, Joan & Vallduví, Enric (2011). A multilingual annotated corpus for the study of information structure. In Marek Konopka, Jacqueline Kubczak, Christian Mair, František Štícha, & Ulrich Hermann Waßner (Eds.) *Grammatik und Korpora 2009 dritte internationale Konferenz Mannheim* (Grammar & Corpora 2009 third international conference) (pp. 305–327). Leibniz-Institut für Deutsche Sprache. https://hdl.handle.net/10230/69342

Brysbaert, Marc, Stevens, Michaël, Mandera, Paweł & Keuleers, Emmanuel (2016). How many words do we know? Practical estimates of vocabulary size dependent on word definition, the degree of language input and the participant's age. *Frontiers in Psychology* 7, 1116. https://doi.org/10.3389/fpsyg.2016.01116

Burnette, Jessie & Calude, Andreea S. (2022). Wake up New Zealand! Directives, politeness and stance in Twitter #Covid19 NZ posts. *Journal of Pragmatics 196*, 6–23. https://doi.org/10.1016/j.pragma.2022.05.002

Burke, Deborah & Shafto, Meredith (2011). Language and aging. In Fergus I. M. Craik, Timothy A. Salthouse (Eds.) *The handbook of aging and cognition* (pp. 373–443). Psychology Press.

Burridge, Kate & Stebbins, Tonya N. (2020). *For the love of Language: An introduction to linguistics*. (2nd Edition). Cambridge University Press.

Calhoun, Kendra & Fawcett, Alexia (2023). "They edited out her nip nops": linguistic innovation as textual censorship avoidance on TikTok. *Language@ Internet 21*, 1–30. https://doi.org/10.14434/li.v21.37371

Calude, Andreea S. (2023). *The linguistics of social media: An introduction*. Routledge.

Cameron, Deborah (2023). *Language, sexism and misogyny*. Routledge.

Carey, James W. (1989). *Communication as culture: Essays on media and society*. Routledge.

Chaffin, Roger & Glass, Arnold (1990). A comparison of hyponym and synonym decisions. *Journal of Psycholinguistic Research 19*, 265–280. https://doi.org/10.1007/BF01077260

Chen, Hui, Xu, Yiru & Guan, Ling (2024). Conversational behaviours in clinical diagnosis: An empirical study of Question–Answering of dementia in Alzheimer-type patients. In Huang Lihe & Boyd Davis (Eds.) *Language, aging and society: What can linguistics do for the aging world*? (pp. 115–138). Nature.

Cheshire, Jenny, Fox, Susan, Kerswill, Paul & Torgesen, Eivind (2013). Language contact and language change in the multicultural metropolis. *Revue française de linguistique appliquée XVIII*(2), 63–76.

Cheshire, Jenny, Fox, Susan Kerswill, Paul & Torgesen, Eivind (2022). Multicultural London English. In Kingsley Bolton (Ed.) *Wiley Blackwell Encyclopedia of World Englishes* (pp. 1–19). Wiley Blackwell.

Christiansen, Morten H. & Chater, Nick (2022). *The language game: How improvisation created language and changed the world*. Random House.

Clark, Eve (2016). *First language acquisition.* (3rd Edition). Cambridge University Press.

Comer, Joseph (2018). Equality on the sea. *Gender and Language 12*(4), 479–503. https://doi.org/10.1558/genl.33353

Crowley, Terry, Lynch, John, Siegel, Jeff & Piau, Julie (1995). *Design of language: An introduction to descriptive linguistics.* Longman.

Crystal, David (2005). *The English language: A guided tour of the language.* Penguin.

Crystal, David (2006). *The fight for English: How language pundits ate, shot, and left.* Oxford University Press.

Crystal, David (2007). *How language works: How babies babble, words change meaning, and languages live or die.* Penguin.

Davis, Jenny L. (2014). Intersections of religion and language revitalization. In Stanley D. Brunn (Ed.) *The changing world religion map: Sacred places, identities, practices and politics* (pp. 1091–1101). Springer.

De Boinod, Adam Jacot (2007). *The meaning of tingo: And other extraordinary words from around the world.* Penguin.

De Cesare, Anna-Maria (2014). Cleft constructions in a contrastive perspective. In Anna-Maria De Cesare (Ed.) *Frequency, forms and functions of cleft constructions in Romance and Germanic* (pp. 9–48). Mouton De Gruyter.

De Deyne, Simon, Brysbaert, Marc & Elgort, Irina (2023). Cross-language influences in L2 semantic and conceptual representation and processing. In Irina Elgort, Anna Siyanova-Chanturia & Marc Brysbaert (Eds.) *Cross-language influences in bilingual processing and second language acquisition* (pp. 152–186). John Benjamins.

DeGraff, Michel (2007). Kreyòl Ayisyen/Haitian Creole. 'Haitian Creole'. In John Holm & Peter Patrick (Eds.) *Comparative Creole syntax: Parallel outlines of 18 Creole grammars* (pp. 101–126). Battlebridge Publications.

DeJesus, Jasmine M., Santhanagopalan, Radhika & Kinzler, Katherine D. (2022). Experimental methods to elicit language attitudes among children. In Ruth Kircher & Lena Zipp (Eds.) *Research methods in language attitudes* (pp. 234–249). Cambridge University Press.

Divjak, Dagmar, Sun, Hui & Milin, Petar (2024). Physiological responses and cognitive behaviours: Measures of heart rate variability index language knowledge. *Journal of Neurolinguistics 69*, 101177.

Dixon, Robert M. (2022). *A new grammar of Dyirbal.* Oxford University Press.

Douce, Wilson (2023). *A corpus-based variationist description of demonstratives in Haitian Creole.* Doctoral dissertation, Aston University.

Dragojevic, Marko, Fasoli, Fabio, Cramer, Jennifer & Rakić, Tamara (2021). Toward a century of language attitudes research: Looking back and moving forward. *Journal of Language and Social Psychology 40*(1), 60–79. https://doi.org/10.1177/0261927X20966714

Dryer, Matthew S. & Haspelmath, Martin (Eds.) (2013). WALS Online (v2020.4) [Data set]. Zenodo. https://doi.org/10.5281/zenodo.13950591 (Available online at https://wals.info).

Duhamel, Marie-France & Meyerhoff, Miriam (2015). An end of egalitarianism? Social evaluations of language difference in New Zealand. *Linguistics Vanguard 1*(1), 235–248. https://doi.org/10.1515/lingvan-2014-1005

Dylman, Alexandra S. & Champoux-Larsson, Marie-France (2020). It's (not) all Greek to me: Boundaries of the foreign language effect. *Cognition 196*, 104148. https://doi.org/10.1016/j.cognition.2019.104148

Eckert, Penelope (1988). Adolescent social structure and the spread of linguistic change. *Language in Society 17*(2), 183–207. https://doi.org/10.1017/S0047404500012756

Ethnologue: languages of the world. (2025). Dallas, Texas, SIL International, https://www.ethnologue.com/insights/how-many-languages-endangered (Accessed 4 February 2026).

Evans, Nick (2022). *Words of wonder: Endangered languages and what they tell us.* John Wiley & Sons.

Fattier, Dominique (2013). Haitian Creole. In Susanne Maria Michaelis, Philippe Maurer, Martin Haspelmath & Magnus Huber (Eds.) *The survey of Pidgin and Creole languages* (pp. 195–204). Oxford University Press.

Fillmore, Charles (1971). *Lectures on Deixis.* University of Michigan.

Fortescue, Michael (2004). West Greenlandic (Eskimo). In Joachim Mugdan, Wolfgang Kesselheim, Stavros Skopeteas, Christain Lehmann, & Geert Booij (Eds.) *Morphologie:* (*Volume Part* 2, pp. 1389–1399). De Gruyter. https://doi.org/10.1515/9783110172782.2.16.1389

Fotiou, Constantina & Grohmann, Kleanthes K. (2022). A small island with big differences? Folk perceptions in the context of dialect levelling and koineization. *Frontiers in Communication 6,* 770088. https://doi.org/10.3389/fcomm.2021.770088

Fought, Carmen & Eisenhauer, Karen (2022). *Language and gender in children's animated films: Exploring Disney and Pixar.* Cambridge University Press.

Fowler, Henry (1926). *Modern English usage.* (4th edition) edited by Jeremy Butterfield in 2015, Oxford University Press.

Gardner, Bill (2014). From 'shrill' housewife to Downing Street: the changing voice of Margaret Thatcher. *Telegraph.* (Accessed on 9 January 2026) https://www.telegraph.co.uk/news/politics/11251919/From-shrill-housewife-to-Downing-Street-the-changing-voice-of-Margaret-Thatcher.html?ICID=continue_without_subscribing_reg_first

Garza, Joyhann Yoo (2021). 'Where all my bad girls at?': Cosmopolitan femininity through racialised appropriations in K-pop. *Gender and Language 15*(1), 11–41. https://doi.org/10.1558/genl.18565

George, Rachel (2020). Simultaneity and the refusal to choose: The semiotics of Serbian youth identity on Facebook. *Language in Society 49*(3), 399–423. https://doi.org/10.1017/S004740451900099X

German Federal Government (2022). *Migration Report of the Federal Government.* (Accessed on 23 January 2026). https://www.bamf.de/SharedDocs/Anlagen/EN/Forschung/Migrationsberichte/migrationsbericht-2022-kurzfassung.pdf?__blob=publicationFile&v=9#:~:text=Humanitarian%20migration%20increased%20again%20for,%3A%2084%2C095%3B%20%2B11.7%25)

Gluszek, Agata & Dovidio, John F. (2010). Speaking with a nonnative accent: Perceptions of bias, communication difficulties, and belonging in the United States. *Journal of language and social psychology 29*(2), 224–234. https://doi.org/10.1177/0261927X09359590

Gordon, Matthew J. (2019). Language variation and change in rural communities. *Annual Review of Linguistics 5*(1), 435–453. https://doi.org/10.1146/annurev-linguistics-011817-045545

Greco, Mateo (2022). From Latin to Modern Italian: Some notes on negation. *Languages* 7(1), 46. https://doi.org/10.3390/languages7010046

Grice, Paul (1989). *Studies in the way of words*. Harvard University Press.

Grosjean, François (2010). *Bilingual: Life and reality*. Harvard University Press.

Gunkel, David J. (2025a). *AI for communication*. Routledge.

Gunkel, David J. (2025b). Prompted by me. Generated by ChatGPT. *Human-Machine Communication 10*(1), 31–42. https://doi.org/10.30658/hmc.10.2

Han, Yanmei (2021). Situated impoliteness revisited: Blunt anti-epidemic slogans and conflicting comments during the coronavirus outbreak in China. *Journal of Pragmatics 178*, 31–42. https://doi.org/10.1016/j.pragma.2021.03.004

Haspelmath, Martin & Sims, Andrea (2010). *Understanding morphology*. Routledge.

Haspelmath, Martin & Tadmor, Uri (Eds.) (2009). *World Loanword Database*. Leipzig. (Available online at https://wold.clld.org, Accessed on 19 December 2025).

Hazenberg, Evan (2020). Can you tell someone's sexuality from the way they speak? In Laurie Bauer & Andreea S. Calude (Eds.) *Questions about language: What everyone should know about language in the 21st century* (pp. 108–122). Routledge.

Hendrikse, Rusandré & Mfusi, Mmemezi (2011). Circumfixes as emergent linguistic structures. *South African Journal of African Languages 31*(1), 41–53. https://doi.org/10.1080/02572117.2011.10587355

Hinrichs, Lars, Szmrecsanyi, Benedikt & Bohmann, Axel (2015). "Which"-hunting and the standard English relative clause. *Language 91*(4), 806–636.

Hirschfeld, Lawrence A. & Gelman, Susan A. (1997). What young children think about the relationship between language variation and social difference. *Cognitive Development 12*(2), 213–238.

Hockett, Charles F. (1960). The origin of speech. *Scientific American 203*, 88–111.

Holmes, Janet, Vine, Bernadette & Johnson, Gary (1998). *The Wellington corpus of Spoken New Zealand English: A users' guide*. School of Linguistics and Applied Language Studies, Victoria University of Wellington.

Huang, Lihe & Davis, Boyd (2024). *Language, aging and society: What can linguistics do for the aging world*? Springer.

Huang, Yan (2013). *Pragmatics*. (2nd edition). Oxford University Press.

Ibbotson, Paul (2022). *Language acquisition: The basics*. Palgrave/Macmillan.

Ilbury, Christian (2020). "Sassy queens": Stylistic orthographic variation in Twitter and the enregisterment of AAVE. *Journal of Sociolinguistics 24*(2), 245–264. https://doi.org/10.1111/josl.12366

Jacquet, Baptiste, Hullin, Alexandre, Baratgin, Jean & Jamet, Frank (2019). The impact of the Gricean maxims of Quality, Quantity and Manner in chatbots. *International Conference on Information and Digital Technologies* (pp. 180–189). Zilina, Slovakia, IEEE. https://doi.org/10.1109/DT.2019.8813473

Jourdan, Christine (2021). Pidgins and creoles: The blurring of categories. *Annual Review of Anthropology 50*, 363–378. https://doi.org/10.1146/annurev-anthro-121319-071304

Kahneman, Daniel (2011). *Thinking, fast and slow*. Farrar, Straus and Giroux.

Kerswill, Paul & Wiese, Heike (2022). *Urban contact dialects and language*. Routledge.

Kim, Jieun (2023). North Korea sentences 20 young athletes for 'speaking like South Koreans'. *Radio Free Asia*. (Accessed on 9 January 2026). https://www.rfa.org/english/news/korea/athletes-04132023094854.html

Kim, Sujin, Jeon, Seong Gak, Nam, Yunkwon, Kim, Hyeon Soo, Yoo, Doo-Han & Moon, Minho (2019). Bilingualism for dementia: Neurological mechanisms associated with functional and structural changes in the brain. *Frontiers in Neuroscience 13*, 1224. https://doi.org/10.3389/fnins.2019.01224

Kishimoto, Reiki & Hashiya, Kazuhide (2025). Recency and rarity effects in disambiguating the focus of utterance: A developmental study. *PloS One 20*(2), e0317433. https://doi.org/10.1371/journal.pone.0317433

Klégr, Aleš (2018). Language is *embiggened* by words that don't exist: The case of a circumfix. *Linguistica Pragensia 28*(1), 53–70.

Konnelly, Lex (2022). Transmedicalism and 'trans enough'. *Gender and Language 16*(1), 1–25. https://doi.org/10.1558/genl.20230

Kuno, Susumo (1973). *The Structure of the Japanese language*. Massachusetts Institute of Technology Press.

Labov, William (2001). *Principles of linguistic change, Vol. 2: Social factors*. Blackwell.

Lakoff, Robin (1973). Language and woman's place. *Language in Society 2*(1), 45–80.

Lambert, Wallace, Hodgson, Richard C., Gardner, Robert & Fillenbaum, Samuel (1960). Evaluational reactions to spoken languages. *The Journal of Abnormal and Social Psychology, 60*(1), 44–51. https://doi.org/10.1037/h0044430

Lenneberg, Eric H. (1967). *Biological foundations of language*. Wiley.

Levinson, Stephen & Brown, Penelope (1987). *Politeness: Some universals in language usage*. Cambridge University Press.

Linell, Per (2019). The written language bias (WLB) in linguistics 40 years after. *Language Sciences 76*, 101230.

Loftus, Elizabeth F. & Zanni, Guido (1975). Eyewitness testimony: The influence of the wording of a question. *Bulletin of the Psychonomic Society 5*(1), 86–88. https://doi.org/10.3758/BF03336715

Lu, Shengwen, Zhao, Qiqi, Guan, Yu, Sun, Zhiwen, Li, Wenhao, Guo, Sifan & Zhang, Aihua (2024). The communication mechanism of the gut-brain axis and its effect on central nervous system diseases: A systematic review. *Biomedicine & Pharmacotherapy 178*, 117207. https://doi.org/10.1016/j.biopha.2024.117207

Matras, Yaron (2009). Defining the limits of grammatical borrowing. In Angela Marcantonio (Ed.) *The Indo-European language family: Questions about its status* (pp. 1–25). Journal of Indo-European Studies Monograph Series, No. 55.

McKee, David & Kennedy, Graham (2000). Lexical comparison of signs from American, Australian, British and New Zealand sign languages. In Karen Emmorey, Harlan L. Lane (Eds.) *The signs of language revisited: An anthology to honor Ursula Bellugi and Edward Klima* (pp. 42–73). Taylor & Francis.

Massaroni, Valentina, Delle Donne, Valentina, Marra, Camillo, Arcangeli, Valentina & Chieffo, Daniela P. R. (2023). The relationship between language and technology: How screen time affects language development in early life—a systematic review. *Brain Sciences 14*(1), 27. https://doi.org/10.3390/brainsci14010027

Michaelis, Susanne Maria, Maurer, Philippe, Haspelmath, Martin & Huber, Magnus (Eds.) (2013). *The atlas of Pidgin and Creole language structures*. Oxford University Press. https://apics-online.info/

Miller, Jim & Calude, Andreea S. (2020). Speaking and writing English. In Bas Aarts, April McMahon & Lars Hinrichs (Eds.) *The Handbook of English Linguistics* (pp. 547–567). Wiley.

Miller, Jim & Weinert, Regina (1998). *Spontaneous spoken language: Syntax and discourse*. Clarendon Press.

Miller, Jim & Weinert, Regina (1998). *Spontaneous spoken language: Syntax and discourse*. Oxford University Press.

Moravcsik, Edith A. (2000). Infixation. In Geert Booij, Christian Lehmann & Joachim Mugdan (Eds.) *Morphologie/Morphology* (pp. 545–551). Walter de Gruyter.

Moravcsik, Edith (2000). Infixation. In Geert E. Booij, Christian Lehmann, Joachim Mugdan, Wolfgang Kesselheim & Stavros Skopeteas (Eds.) *Morphology: An international handbook on inflection and word-formation 1* (pp. 545–552) Mouton de Gruyter.

Moravcsik, Edith (2006). *An introduction to syntax: Fundamentals of syntactic analysis*. Bloomsbury.

Needle, Jeremy M. & Tagliamonte, Sali A. (2025). *Buddies*, *Dudes*, and *Bros* of Ontario: Trends and patterns of vocative change. *Journal of English Linguistics 53*, 00754242251341318. https://doi.org/10.1177/00754242251341318

Norrman, Gunnar (2024). Reconceptualizing the critical period hypothesis for second language acquisition: An appraisal of Lenneberg's work on the epigenesis of language. *Language Sciences 105*, 101645. https://doi.org/10.1016/j.langsci.2024.101645

Ogiermann, Eva (2025). "Stay safe!"—A wish, advice, or an order? Pragmatic variability and change in times of a pandemic. *Journal of Historical Pragmatics 26*(3), 321–353. https://doi.org/10.1075/jhp.23029.ogi

Online Etymology Dictionary (n.d.). "bistro (n.)", https://www.etymonline.com/word/bistro [Accessed 30 Dec 2025], "semantics", https://www.etymonline.com/search?q=semantics [Accessed 30 Dec 2025]

Onysko, Alexander (2017). Conceptual metaphor variation in meaning interpretation: Evidence from speakers of New Zealand English. *Cognitive Linguistic Studies 4*(1), 7–35. https://doi.org/10.1075/cogls.4.1.02ony

Oyebola, Folajimi & Ugwuanyi, Kingsley (2023). Attitudes of Nigerians towards BBC Pidgin: A preliminary study. *Language Matters 54*(1), 78–101. https://doi.org/10.1080/10228195.2023.2203509

Perkins, Emily (2023). *Lioness*. Bloomsbury.

Pivac Alexander, Sara & Major, George (2020). Is learning a signed language easier than learning a spoken language? In Laurie Bauer & Andreea S. Calude (Eds.) *Questions about language: What everyone should know about language in the 21st century* (pp. 123–136). Routledge.

Polyanskaya, Leona, Skopeteas, Stavros, Halama, Peter, Hollenbach, Robin & Ordin, Mikhail (2024). Derivational morphology and suffixing bias on linguistic and nonlinguistic material. *Journal of Language Evolution 9*(1–2), 67–83. https://doi.org/10.1093/jole/lzae005

Preston, David R. (1981). Perceptual dialectology: Mental maps of United States dialects from a Hawaiian perspective (summary). In Henry Warkentyne (Ed.) *Papers from the 4th International Conference on Methods in Dialectology* (pp. 192–198). University ofVictoria.

Pullum, Geoffrey K. (1989). The great Eskimo vocabulary hoax. *Natural Language & Linguistic Theory* 7(2), 275–281.

Pullum, Geoffrey K. (2009). 50 years of stupid grammar advice. *The Chronicle of Higher Education 55*(32), B15.

Puzar, Aljosa & Hong, Yewon (2018). Korean cuties: Understanding performed winsomeness (aegyo) in South Korea. *The Asia Pacific Journal of Anthropology 19*(4), 333–349. https://doi.org/10.1080/14442213.2018.1477826

Sankoff, Gillian (2018). Language change across the lifespan. *Annual Review of Linguistics 4*(1), 297–316. https://doi.org/10.1146/annurev-linguistics-011817-045438

Schweinberger, Martin & Burridge, Kate (2025a). Vulgarity in online discourse around the English-speaking world. *Lingua 321*, 103946. https://doi.org/10.1016/j.lingua.2025.103946

Schweinberger, Martin & Burridge, Kate (2025b). 201 ways to say 'fuck': What 1.7 billion words of online text shows about how the world swears. *The Conversation*. https://doi.org/10.64628/AA.un7h5q7ev

Seargeant, Philip (2024). *The future of language*. Bloomsbury.

Shannon, Claude E. (1948). A mathematical theory of communication. *The Bell System Technical Journal 27*(3), 379–423. https://doi.org/10.1002/j.1538-7305.1948.tb01338.x

Sharifian, Farzad (2002). Processing hyponymy in L1 and L2. *Journal of Psycholinguistic Research 31*(4), 421–426. https://doi.org/10.1023/A:1019526009927

Shin, Naomi L. (2013). Women as leaders of language change: A qualification from the bilingual perspective. In Ana M. Carvalho & Sara Beaudrie (Eds.) *Selected proceedings of the 6th Workshop on Spanish Sociolinguistics* (pp. 135–147). Cascadilla Proceedings Project.

Skirgård, Hedvig, Hannah J. Haynie, Damián E. Blasi, Harald Hammarström, Jeremy Collins, Jay J. Latarche, Jakob Lesage, Tobias Weber, Alena Witzlack-Makarevich, Sam Passmore, Angela Chira, Luke Maurits, Russell Dinnage, Michael Dunn, Ger Reesink, Ruth Singer, Claire Bowern, Patience Epps, Jane Hill, Outi Vesakoski, Martine Robbeets, Noor Karolin Abbas, Daniel Auer, Nancy A. Bakker, Giulia Barbos, Robert D. Borges, Swintha Danielsen, Luise Dorenbusch, Ella Dorn, John Elliott, Giada Falcone, Jana Fischer, Yustinus Ghanggo Ate, Hannah Gibson, Hans-Philipp Göbel,

Jemima A. Goodall, Victoria Gruner, Andrew Harvey, Rebekah Hayes, Leonard Heer, Roberto E. Herrera Miranda, Nataliia Hübler, Biu Huntington-Rainey, Jessica K. Ivani, Marilen Johns, Erika Just, Eri Kashima, Carolina Kipf, Janina V. Klingenberg, Nikita König, Aikaterina Koti, Richard G. A. Kowalik, Olga Krasnoukhova, Nora L.M. Lindvall, Mandy Lorenzen, Hannah Lutzenberger, Tônia R.A. Martins, Celia Mata German, Suzanne van der Meer, Jaime Montoya Samamé, Michael Müller, Saliha Muradoglu, Kelsey Neely, Johanna Nickel, Miina Norvik, Cheryl Akinyi Oluoch, Jesse Peacock, India O.C. Pearey, Naomi Peck, Stephanie Petit, Sören Pieper, Mariana Poblete, Daniel Prestipino, Linda Raabe, Amna Raja, Janis Reimringer, Sydney C. Rey, Julia Rizaew, Eloisa Ruppert, Kim K. Salmon, Jill Sammet, Rhiannon Schembri, Lars Schlabbach, Frederick W. P. Schmidt, Amalia Skilton, Wikaliler Daniel Smith, Hilário de Sousa, Kristin Sverredal, Daniel Valle, Javier Vera, Judith Voß, Tim Witte, Henry Wu, Stephanie Yam, Jingting Ye 葉婧婷, Maisie Yong, Tessa Yuditha, Roberto Zariquiey, Robert Forkel, Nicholas Evans, Stephen C. Levinson, Martin Haspelmath, Simon J. Greenhill, Quentin D. Atkinson & Russell D. Gray (2023). Grambank reveals the importance of genealogical constraints on linguistic diversity and highlights the impact of language loss. *Science Advances 9*(16), eadg6175. https://www.science.org/doi/10.1126/sciadv.adg6175

Şimşek, Yazgül & Wiese, Heike (2022). Germany: Kiezdeutsch. In Paul Kerswill & Heike Weise (Eds.) *Urban contact dialects and language change* (pp. 300–321). Routledge.

Šipka, Danko (2019). *Lexical layers of identity: Words, meaning, and culture in the Slavic languages*. Cambridge University Press.

Smith, Geoff P. & Siegel, Jeff. (2013). Tok Pisin structure dataset. In Susanne Maria Michaelis, Philippe Maurer, Martin Haspelmath & Magnus Huber (Eds.) *Atlas of Pidgin and Creole language structures online*. Max Planck Institute for Evolutionary Anthropology. (Available from https://apics-online.info/contributions/22, Accessed on 12 January 2026)

Song, Lu (2024). Linguistic studies on persons with Dementia (1993–2023): A bibliometric analysis. In Lihe Huang & Boyd Davis (Eds.) *Language, aging and society: What can linguistics do for the aging world?* (pp. 169–194). Palgrave Macmillan.

Stollznow, Karen (2024). *Bitch: The journey of a word*. Cambridge University Press.

Strunk, William & White, Elwyn Brooks (1999). *The elements of style*. Longman.

Tomasello, Michael (1992). *First verbs: A case study of early grammatical development*. Cambridge University Press.

Treffers-Daller, Jeanine & Calude, Andreea (2015). The role of statistical learning in the acquisition of motion event construal in a second language. *International Journal of Bilingual Education and Bilingualism 18*(5), 602–623. https://doi.org/10.1080/13670050.2015.1027146

Turing, Alan (1950). Computing machinery and intelligence. *Mind, 59*(236), 433–460.

Vance, Andrea (2025). Brooke van Velden drops C-word in Parliament. *Radio New Zealand New*. 14 May. (Accessed 9 January 2026). https://www.rnz.co.nz/news/political/560988/brooke-van-velden-drops-c-word-in-parliament

Wei, Rining, Chen, Jinxian & Wang, Jing (2024). Learning a *Lx* among older adults. In Lihe Huang & Boyd Davis (Eds.) *Language, aging and society: What can linguistics do for the aging world?* (pp. 247–278). Palgrave Macmillan.

White, E. B. & Strunk, William (2023). *The elements of style*. Open Road Media.

Wiese, Heike (2009). Grammatical innovation in multiethnic urban Europe: New linguistic practices among adolescents. *Lingua 119*(5), 782–806. https://doi.org/10.1016/j.lingua.2008.11.002

Winter, Bodo, Perlman, Marcus, Perry, Lynn K. & Lupyan, Gary (2017). Which words are most iconic? Iconicity in English sensory words. *Interaction Studies 18*(3), 443–464. https://doi.org/10.1075/is.18.3.07win

Wiese, Heike (2015). "This migrants' babble is not a German dialect!": The interaction of standard language ideology and 'us'/'them' dichotomies in the public discourse on a multiethnolect. *Language in Society 44*(3), 341–368. https://doi.org/10.1017/S0047404515000226

Zhang, Y. Charles & Schwarz, Norbert (2020). Truth from familiar turns of phrase: Word and number collocations in the corpus of language influence acceptance of novel claims. *Journal of Experimental Social Psychology 90*, 103999. https://doi.org/10.1016/j.jesp.2020.103999

Zipf, George K. (1936). *The psychobiology of language*. Routledge.

INDEX OF LANGUAGES

INDEX OF TOPICS

For Product Safety Concerns and Information please contact our EU representative GPSR@taylorandfrancis.com
Taylor & Francis Verlag GmbH, Kaufingerstraße 24, 80331 München, Germany

www.ingramcontent.com/pod-product-compliance
Lightning Source LLC
LaVergne TN
LVHW050346200826
846010LV00033B/389
* 9 7 8 1 0 4 1 0 2 9 2 2 9 *